EASY PIANO

POP SONGS
IN EASY KEYS

"Pop Songs in Easy Keys" includes no more than one sharp or one flat in the **key signature**.
The key signature appears on the left side of every staff, right next to the clef signs.

no sharps or flats

one sharp: F#
all Fs are played as F#

one flat: B♭
all Bs are played as B♭

Sometimes **accidentals** appear. Accidentals are sharps and flats not in the key signature.
An accidental alters a specific note in a particular measure. The next bar line or a
natural sign (♮) cancels an accidental.

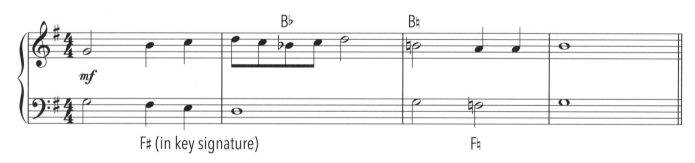

F# (in key signature)

F♮

ISBN 978-1-70517-479-1

7777 W. BLUEMOUND RD. P.O. BOX 13819 MILWAUKEE, WI 53213

Visit Hal Leonard Online at
www.halleonard.com

World headquarters, contact:
Hal Leonard
7777 West Bluemound Road
Milwaukee, WI 53213
Email: info@halleonard.com

In Europe, contact:
Hal Leonard Europe Limited
1 Red Place
London, W1K 6PL
Email: info@halleonardeurope.com

In Australia, contact:
Hal Leonard Australia Pty. Ltd.
4 Lentara Court
Cheltenham, Victoria, 3192 Australia
Email: info@halleonard.com.au

ALL MY LOVING

Words and Music by JOHN LENNON
and PAUL McCARTNEY

Moderately fast

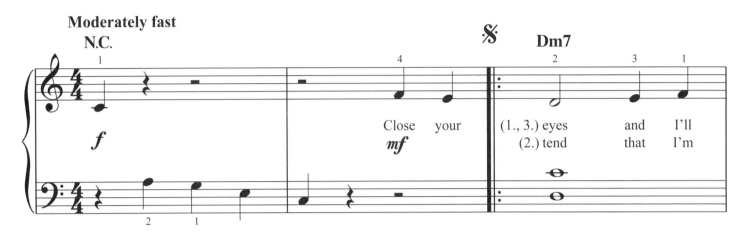

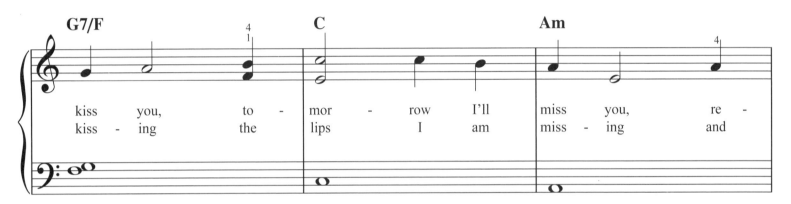

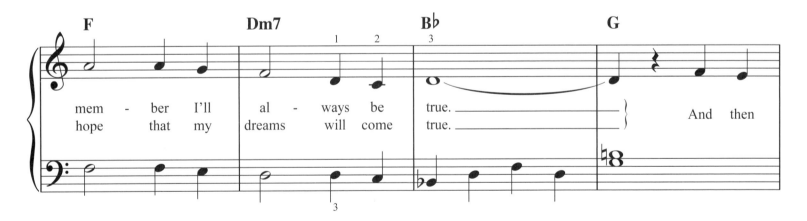

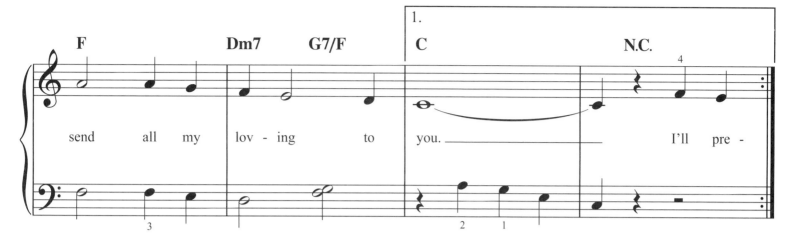

send all my lov - ing to you._____ I'll pre -

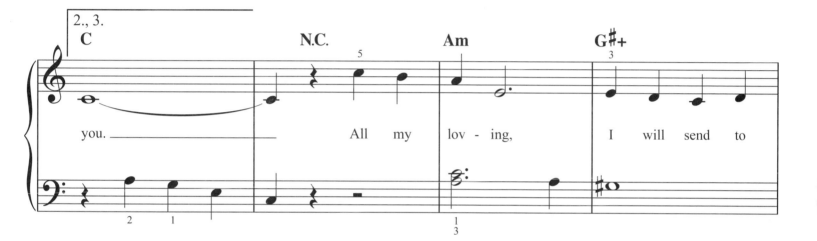

you._____ All my lov - ing, I will send to

you._____ All my lov - ing, dar - ling, I'll be

true. Close your

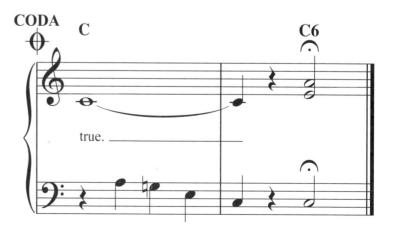

true._____

ALL STAR

Words and Music by
GREG CAMP

Hey now, you're an all star; get your game on, go _____ play.

Hey now, you're a rock star; get the show on, get ___ paid. And all that glit-ters is gold. ___

___ On - ly shoot - in' stars ___ break the mold. _____ It's a

cool place and they say it gets cold-er. You're bun-dled up now; wait till you get old-er. But the

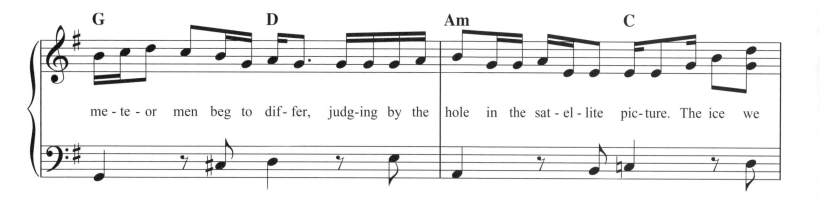

me-te-or men beg to dif-fer, judg-ing by the hole in the sat-el-lite pic-ture. The ice we

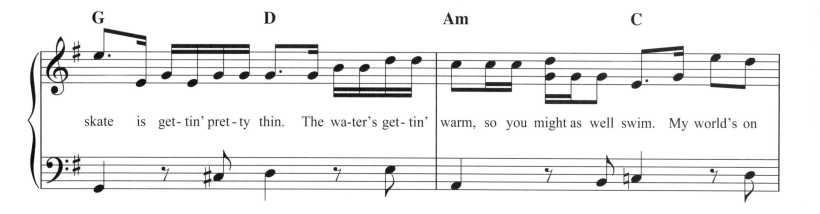

skate is get-tin' pret-ty thin. The wa-ter's get-tin' warm, so you might as well swim. My world's on

fi-re; how 'bout yours? That's the way I like it and I'll nev-er get bored.

BAD DAY

Words and Music by
DANIEL POWTER

Moderately

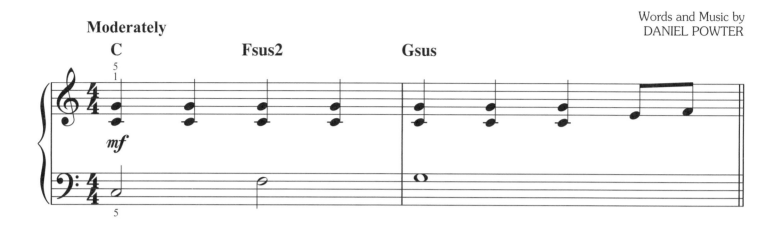

Where is the mo - ment we need - ed the most? _____

You kick up the leaves and the mag - ic is lost. _____

They tell me your blue skies fade to grey. They tell me your pas - sion's gone a -

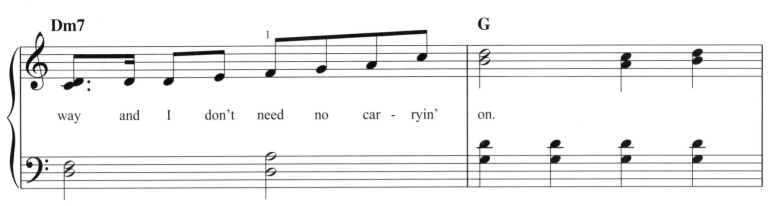

way   and   I   don't   need   no   car - ryin'   on.

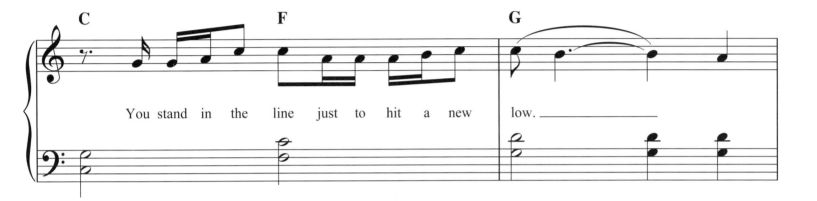

You   stand   in   the   line   just   to   hit   a   new   low. _____

You're   fak - in'   the   smile   with   the   cof - fee   to   go. ____

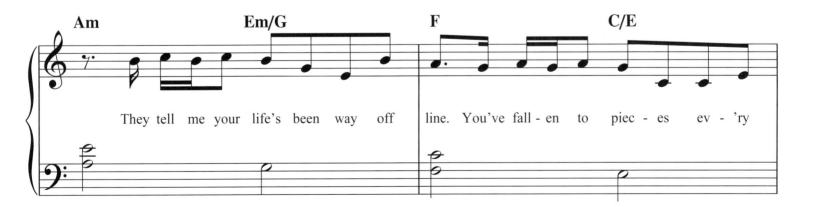

They   tell   me   your   life's   been   way   off   line.   You've   fall - en   to   piec - es   ev - 'ry

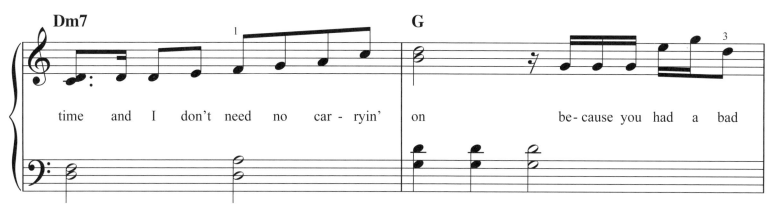

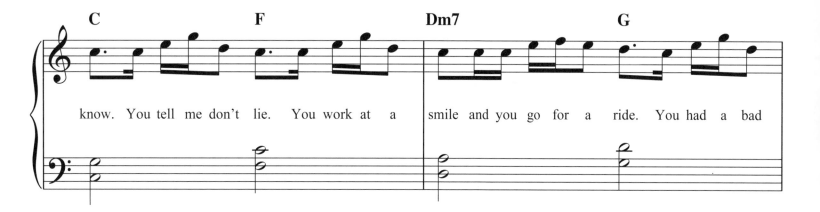

day. _____ You had a bad day.

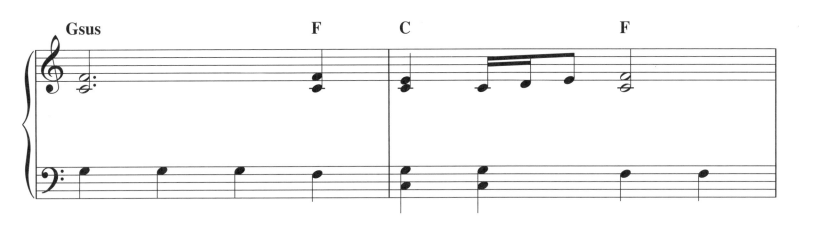

Well, you need a blue sky hol - i -

day. The point is they laugh at what you say and I don't need no car - ryin'

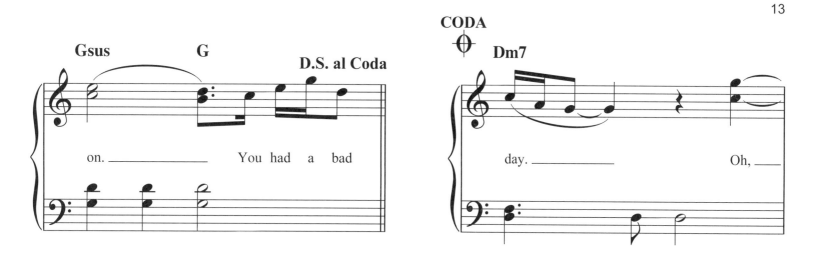

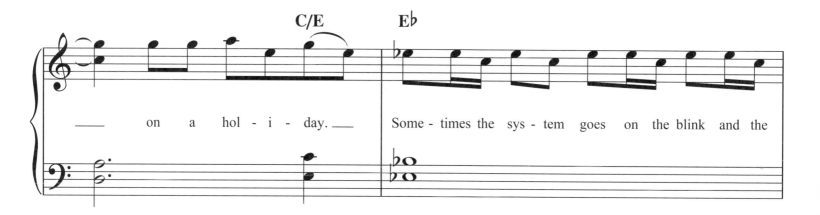

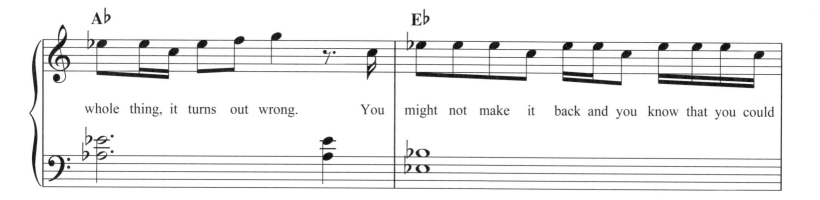

14

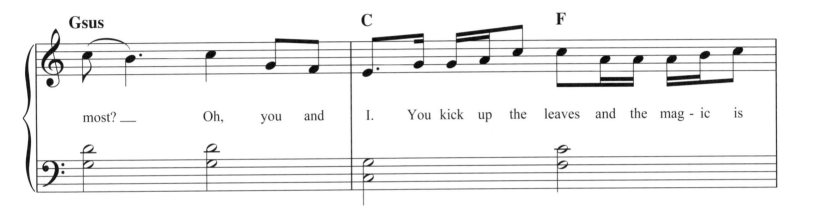

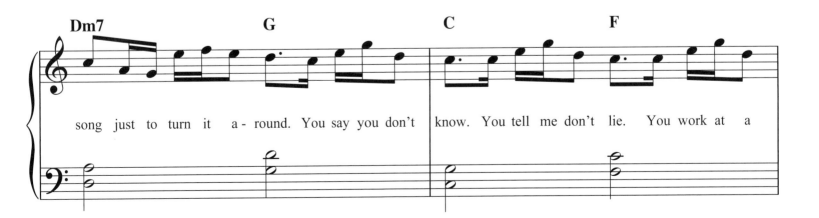

smile and you go for a ride. You had a bad | day. You've seen what you like. And how does it

feel one more time? You had a bad | day. _____ You had a bad

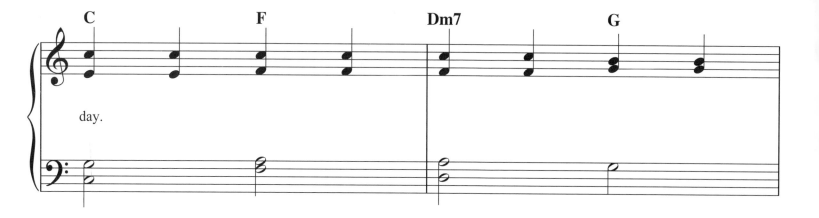

day.

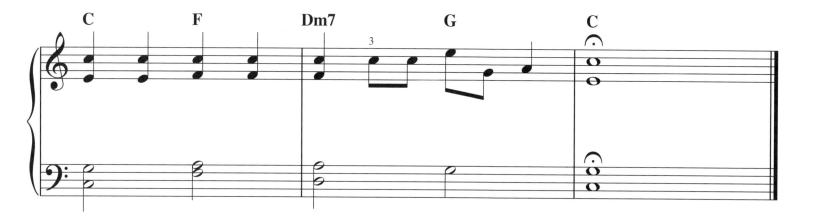

day.

BILLIE JEAN

Words and Music by
MICHAEL JACKSON

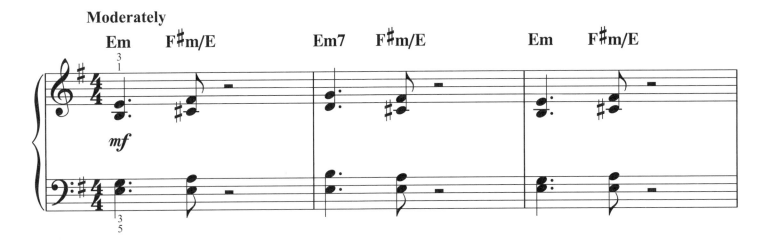

She was more like a beau - ty queen from a mov - ie scene.
For for - ty days and for for - ty nights, law was on her side.

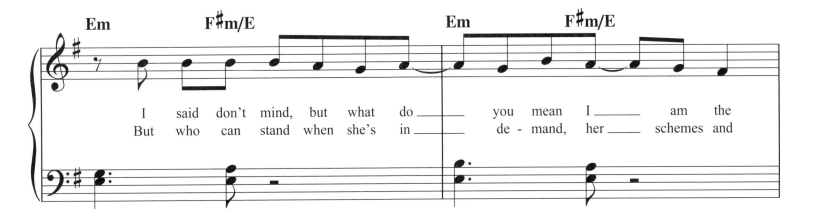

I said don't mind, but what do _____ you mean I _____ am the
But who can stand when she's in _____ de - mand, her _____ schemes and

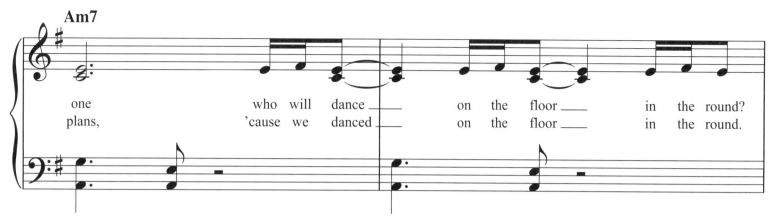

Am7

one   who will dance ____ on the floor ____ in the round?
plans,   'cause we danced ____ on the floor ____ in the round.

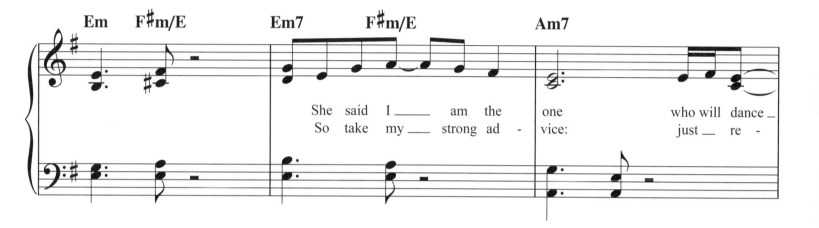

Em   **F♯m/E**   **Em7**   **F♯m/E**   **Am7**

She said I ____ am the   one   who will dance _
So take my ___ strong ad - vice: just _ re -

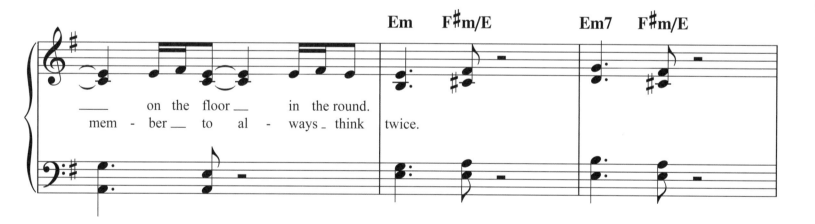

                          Em   **F♯m/E**   **Em7**   **F♯m/E**

____ on the floor ___ in the round.
mem - ber ___ to al - ways _ think   twice.

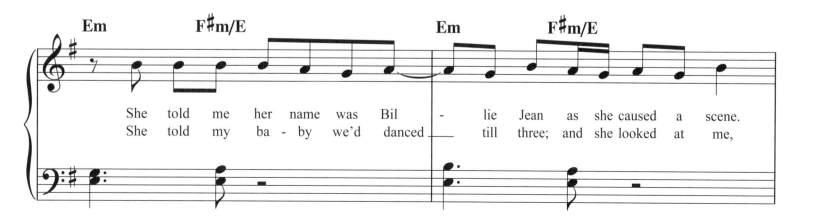

Em   **F♯m/E**   **Em**   **F♯m/E**

She told me her name was Bil - lie Jean as she caused a scene.
She told my ba - by we'd danced ____ till three; and she looked at me,

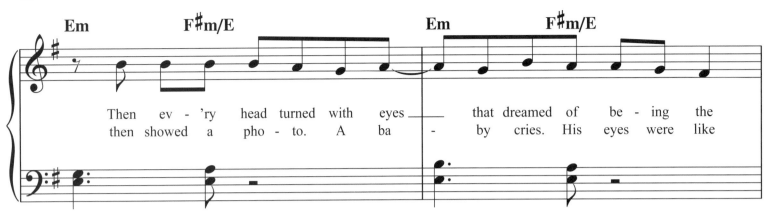

Then ev - 'ry head turned with eyes ___ that dreamed of be - ing the
then showed a pho - to. A ba - by cries. His eyes were like

one who will dance ___ on the floor ___ in the round.
mine. Can we dance ___ on the floor ___ in the round?

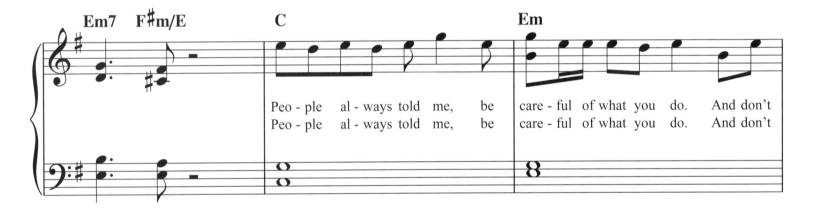

Peo - ple al - ways told me, be care - ful of what you do. And don't
Peo - ple al - ways told me, be care - ful of what you do. And don't

go a - round break - in' young girls' hearts. ___ And
go a - round break - in' young girls' hearts. ___ But you

Moth - er al - ways told me, be
came and stood right by me, just a

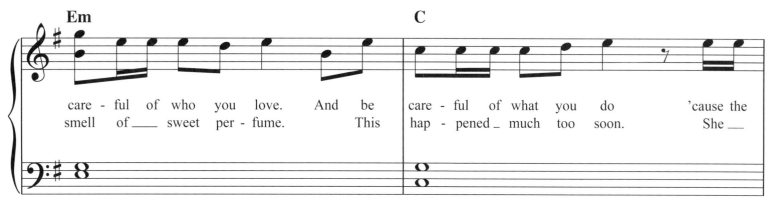

care - ful of who you love. And be care - ful of what you do 'cause the
smell of ___ sweet per - fume. This hap - pened ___ much too soon. She ___

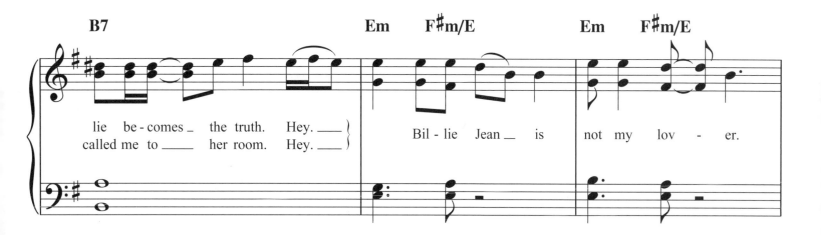

lie be - comes ___ the truth. Hey. ___
called me to ___ her room. Hey. ___

Bil - lie Jean ___ is not my lov - er.

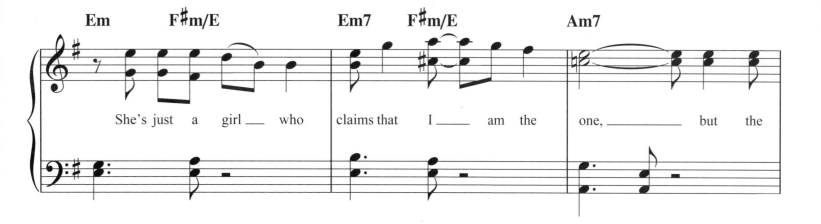

She's just a girl ___ who claims that I ___ am the one, _____ but the

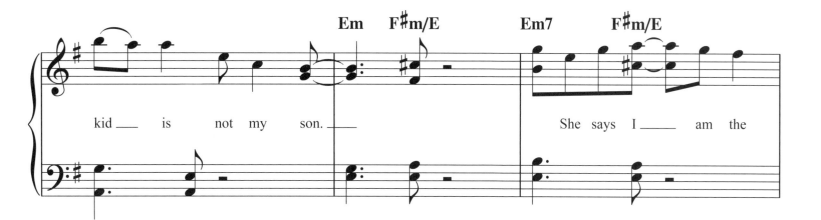

kid ___ is not my son. ___ She says I ___ am the

one, _____ but the kid ___ is not my son.

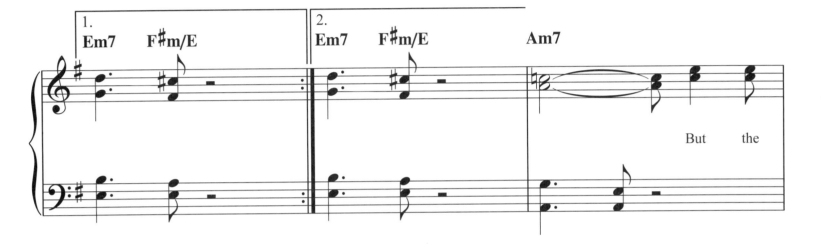

But the

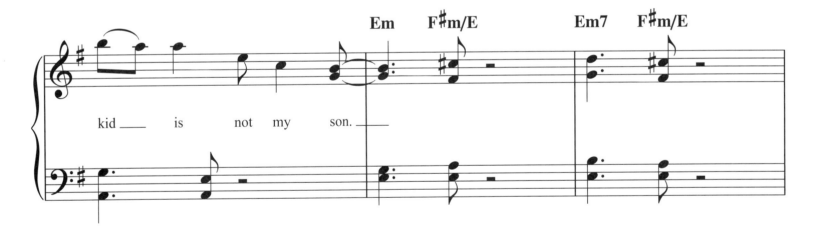

kid ___ is not my son. ___

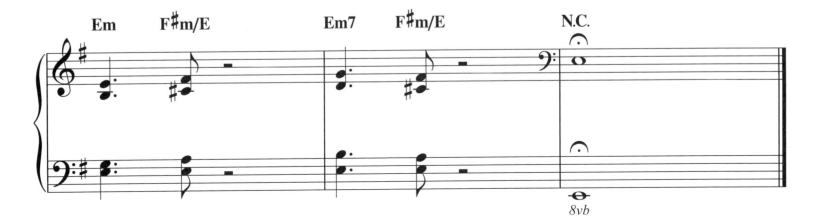

BOHEMIAN RHAPSODY

Words and Music by
FREDDIE MERCURY

Slowly, steady tempo

Ma - ma _____ just

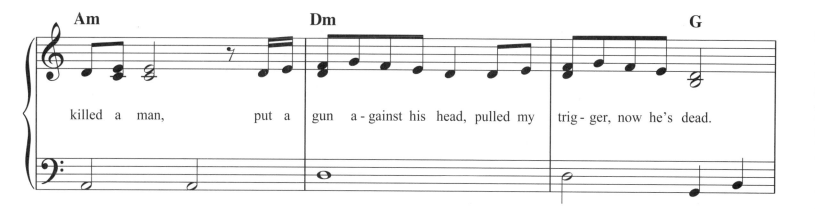

killed a man, put a gun a - gainst his head, pulled my trig - ger, now he's dead.

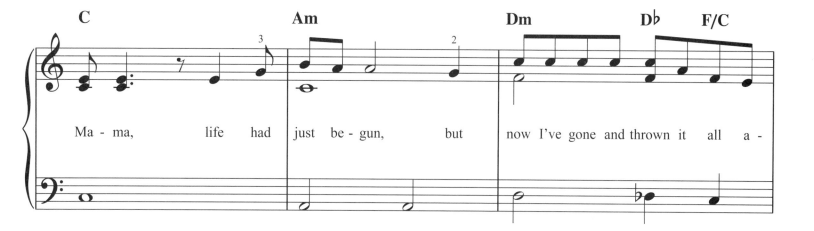

Ma - ma, life had just be - gun, but now I've gone and thrown it all a -

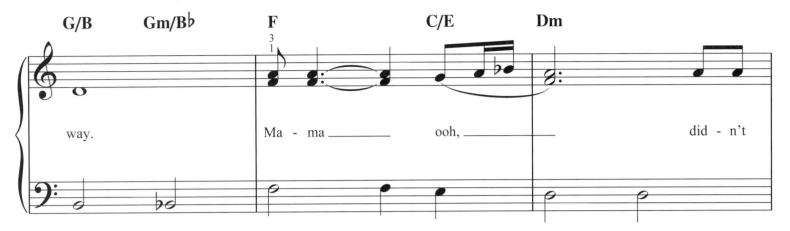

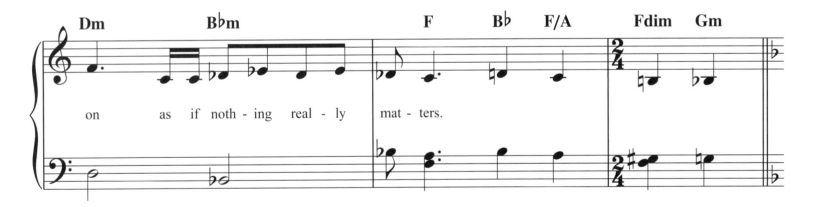

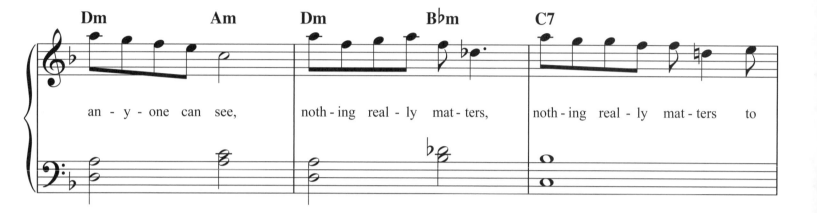

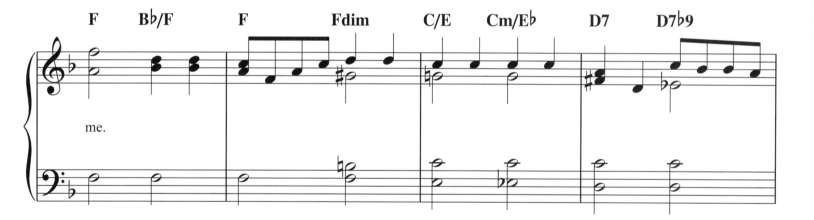

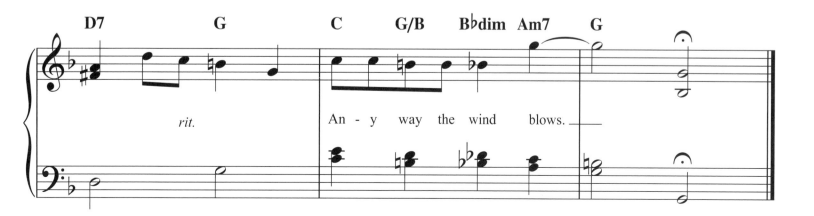

DANCING QUEEN

Words and Music by BENNY ANDERSSON,
BJÖRN ULVAEUS and STIG ANDERSON

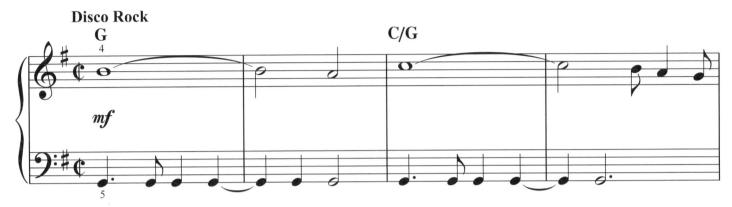

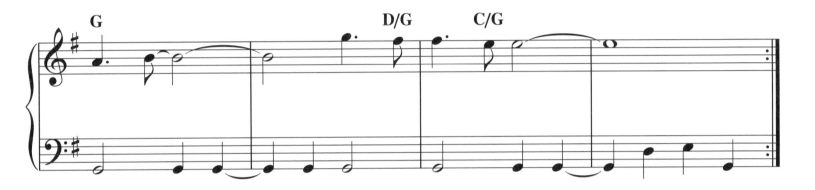

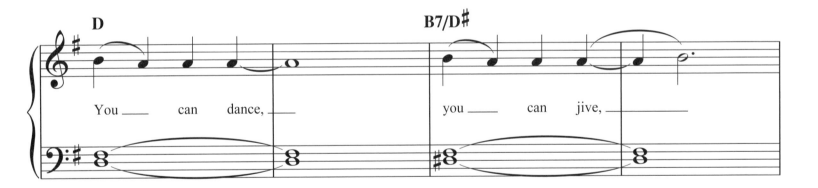

You ___ can dance, ___ you ___ can jive, ___

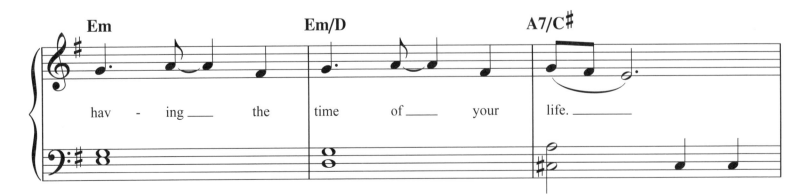

hav - ing ___ the time of ___ your life. ___

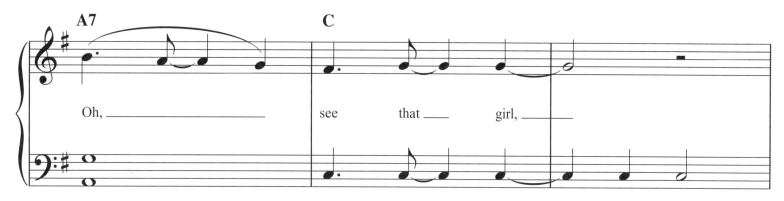

Oh, _____ see that ___ girl, _____

watch that ___ scene, _____ dig - gin' the danc - ing ___ queen.

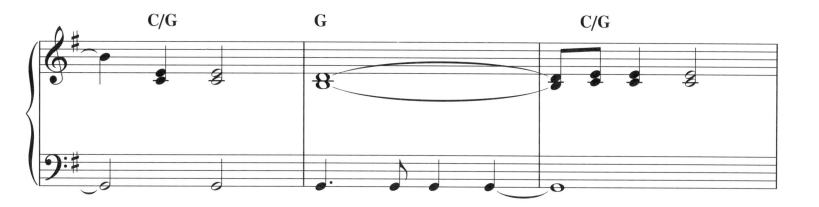

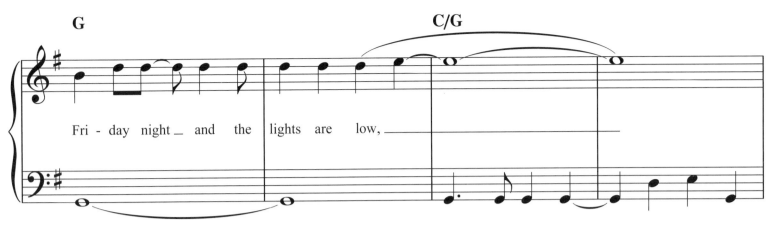

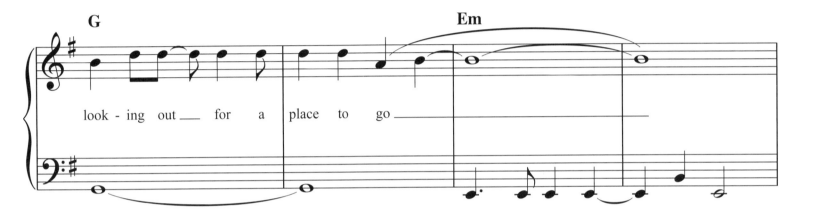

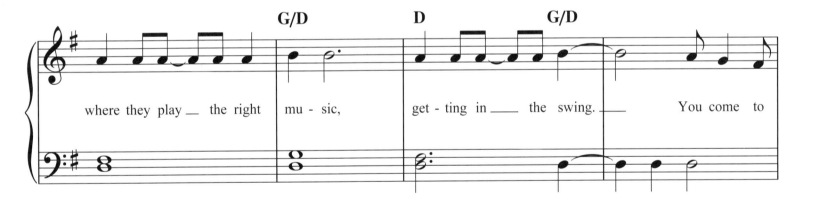

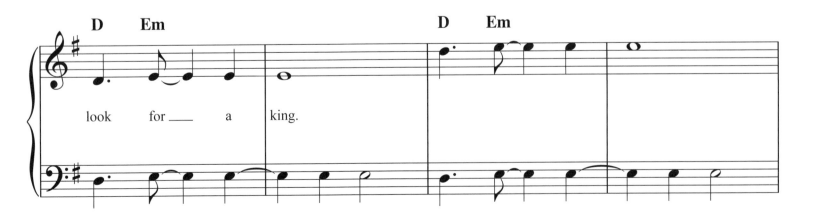

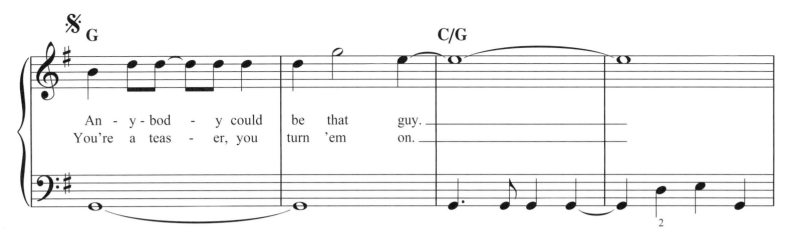

An - y - bod - y could be that guy.
You're a teas - er, you turn 'em on.

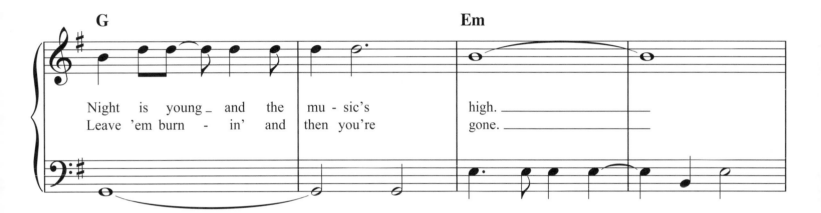

Night is young and the mu - sic's high.
Leave 'em burn - in' and then you're gone.

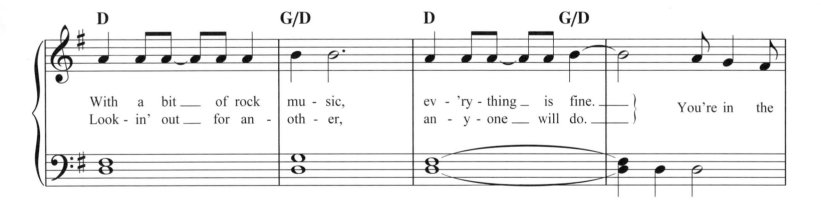

With a bit of rock mu - sic, ev - 'ry - thing is fine.
Look - in' out for an - oth - er, an - y - one will do.
You're in the

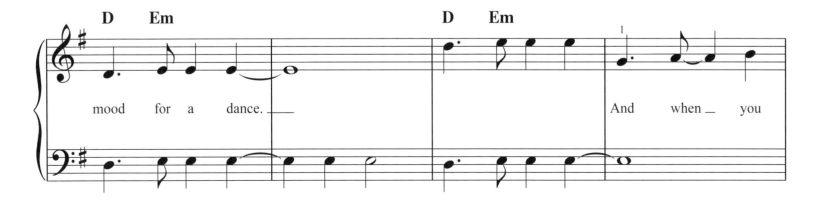

mood for a dance.
And when you

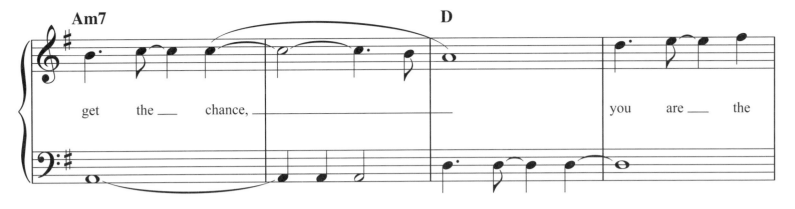

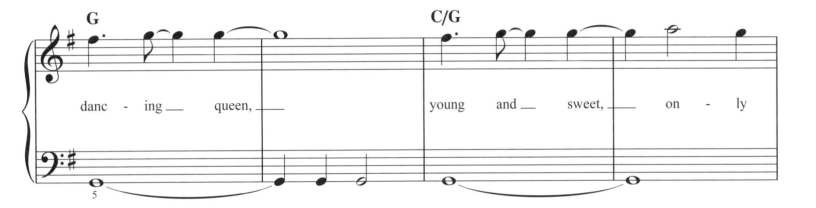

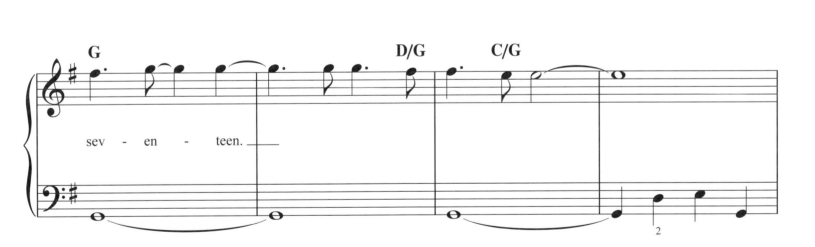

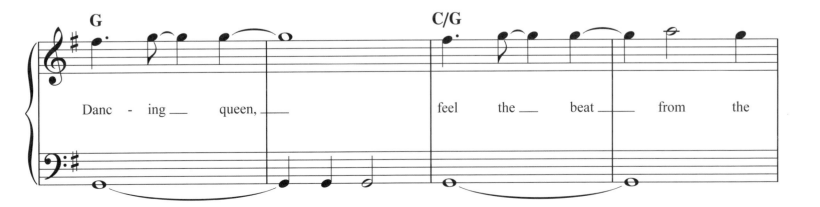

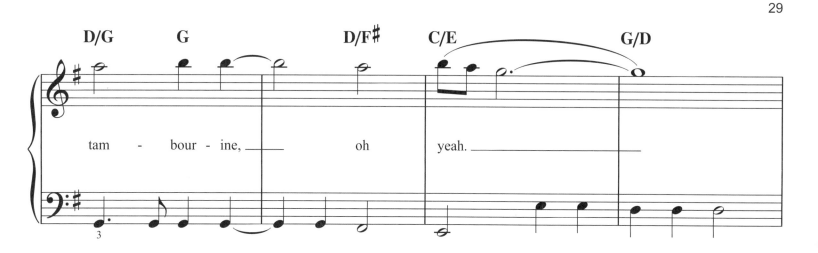

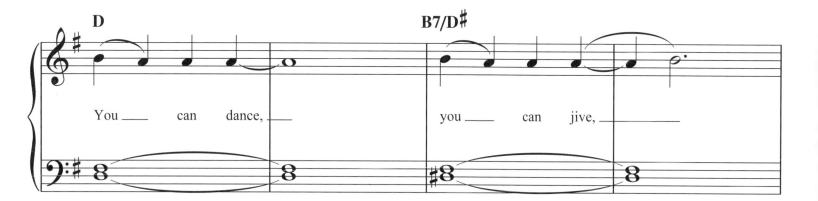

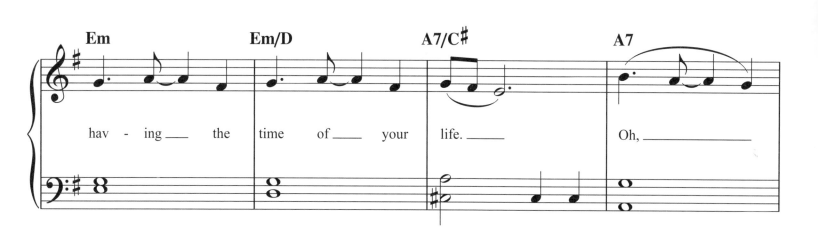

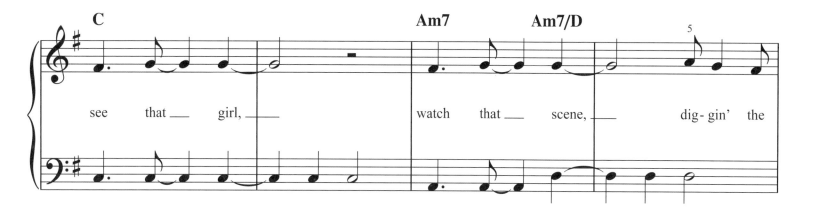

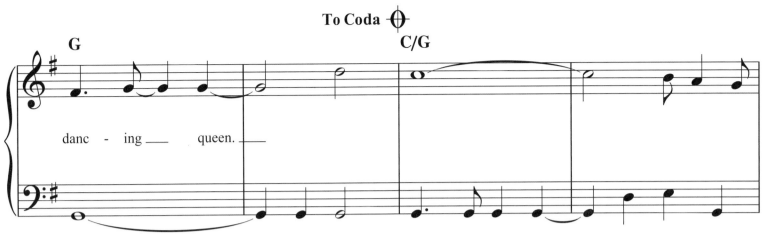

danc - ing ___ queen. ___

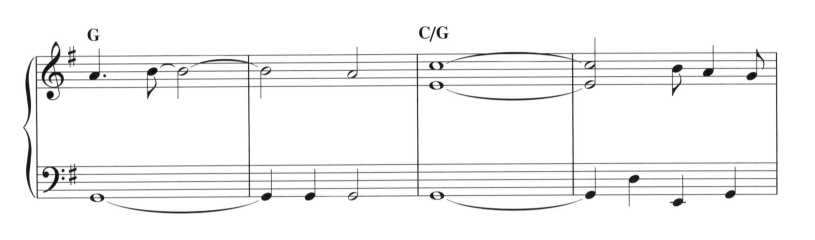

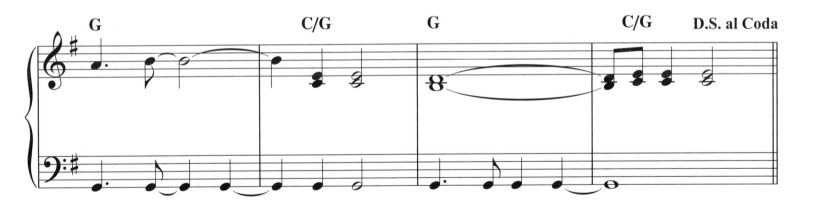

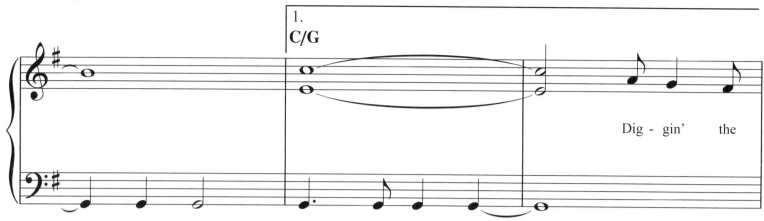

(Everything I Do)
I DO IT FOR YOU
from the Motion Picture ROBIN HOOD: PRINCE OF THIEVES

Words and Music by BRYAN ADAMS,
R.J. LANGE and MICHAEL KAMEN

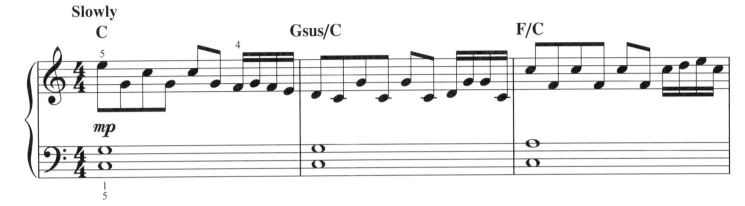

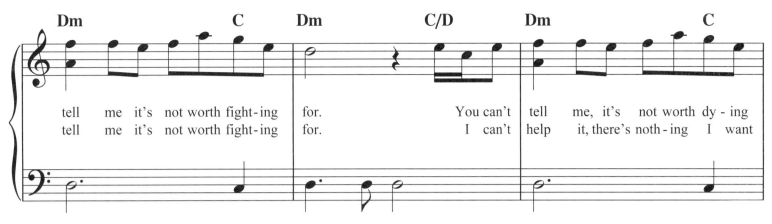

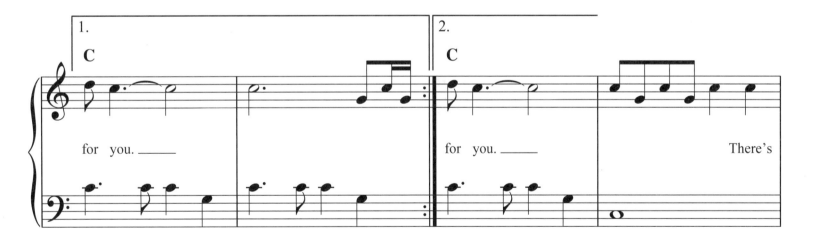

more ____ love. There's no ____ way, ____ un - less you're ____ there all the

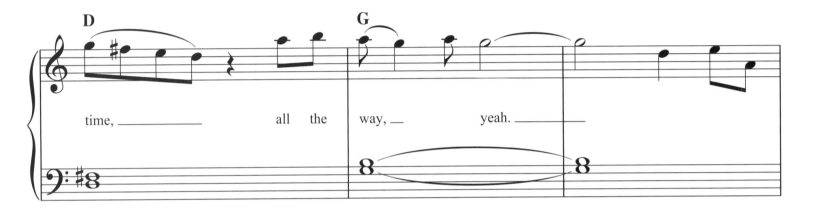

time, _____ all the way, ____ yeah. ____

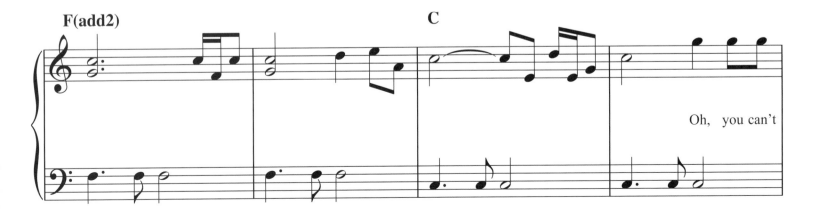

Oh, you can't

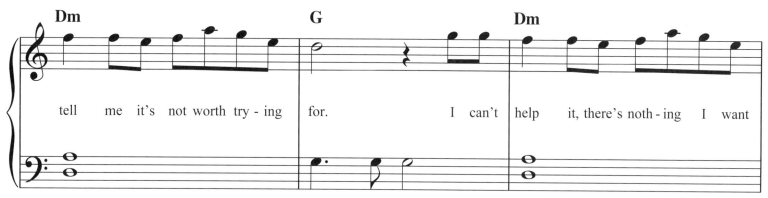

tell me it's not worth try-ing for. I can't help it, there's noth-ing I want

more. Yeah, I would fight __ for you, __ I'd lie ____ for you, __ walk the

wire for you, yeah, I'd die for you. __ You know it's true, ev-'ry-thing I

do, oh, _____ oh, I do it for ___ you.

EYE OF THE TIGER
Theme from ROCKY III

Words and Music by FRANK SULLIVAN
and JIM PETERIK

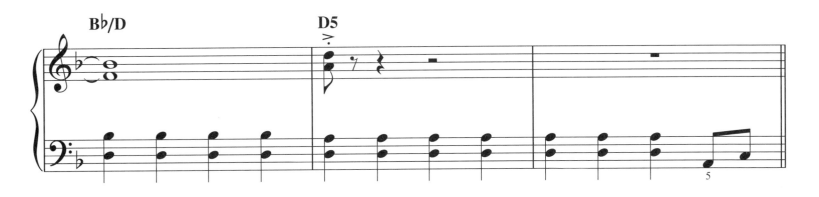

1. Ris - in' up
2. So man - y times it
3.-4. *(See additional lyrics)*

back on the street, _____

hap-pens too fast. _____

did my time, took my
You trade your pas - sion for

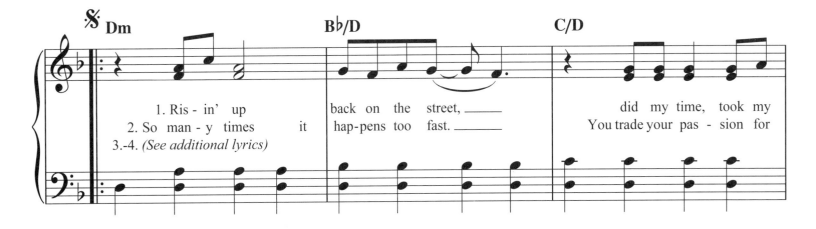

chanc - es.
glo - ry.

Went the dis - tance. Now I'm
Don't lose your grip _____ on the

back on my feet, just a
dreams of the past. You must

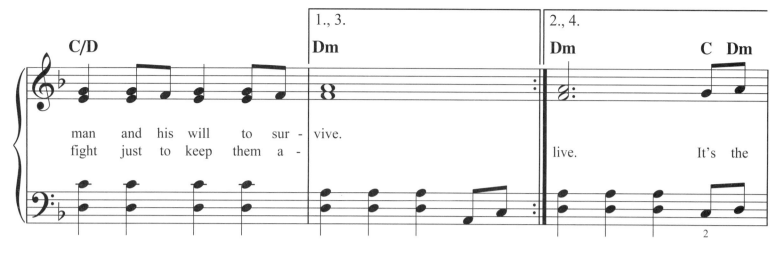

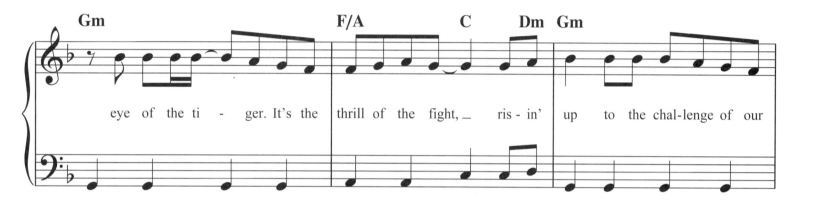

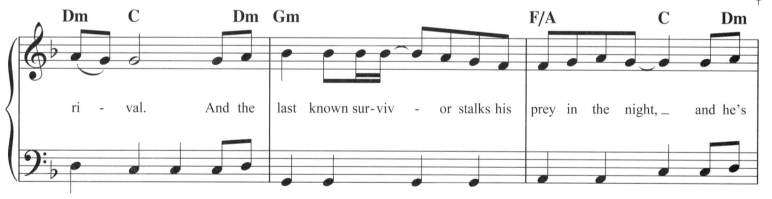

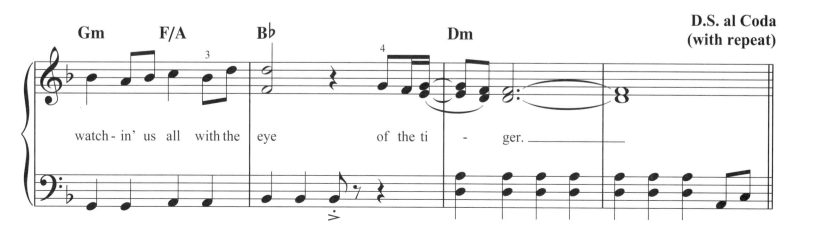

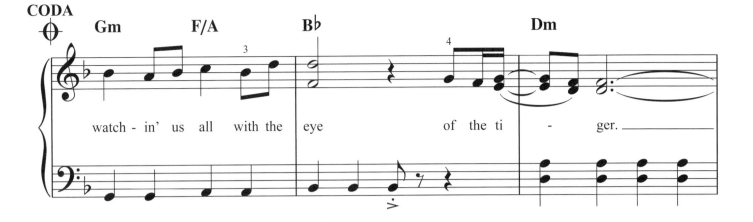

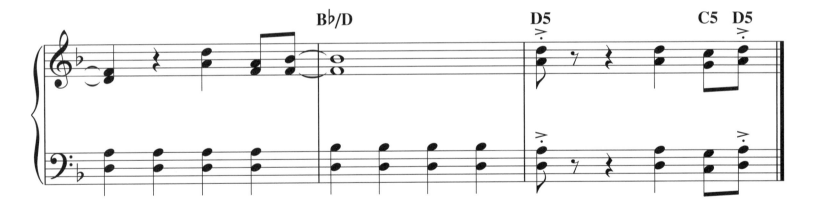

Additional Lyrics

3. Face to face, out in the heat,
   Hangin' tough, stayin' hungry.
   They stack the odds, still we take to the street
   For the kill with the skill to survive.

4. Risin' up, straight to the top.
   Had the guts, got the glory.
   Went the distance. Now I'm not gonna stop,
   Just a man and his will to survive.

I GOTTA FEELING

Words and Music by WILL ADAMS,
ALLAN PINEDA, JAIME GOMEZ,
STACY FERGUSON, DAVID GUETTA
and FREDERIC RIESTERER

Moderately fast

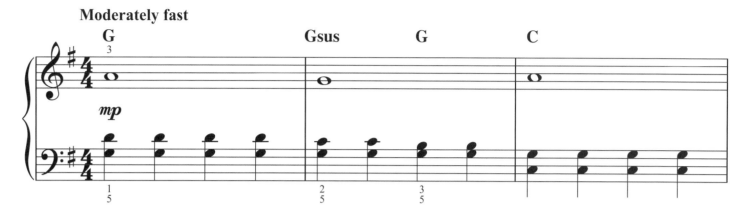

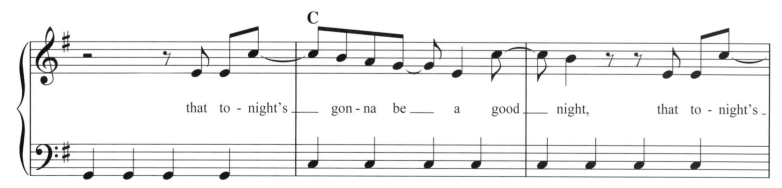

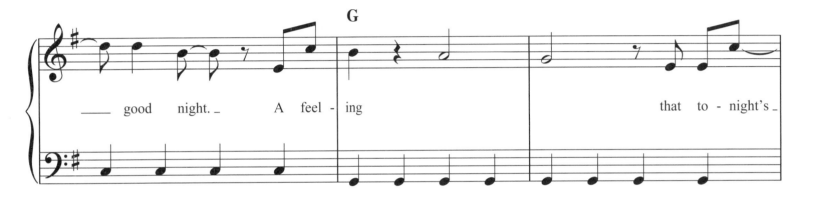

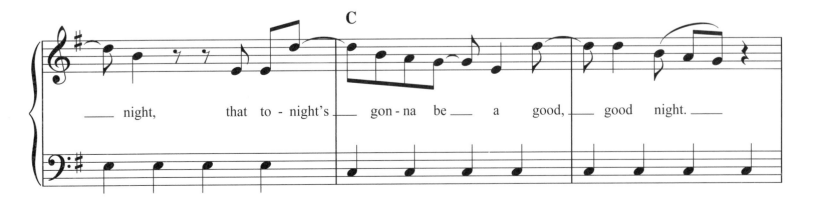

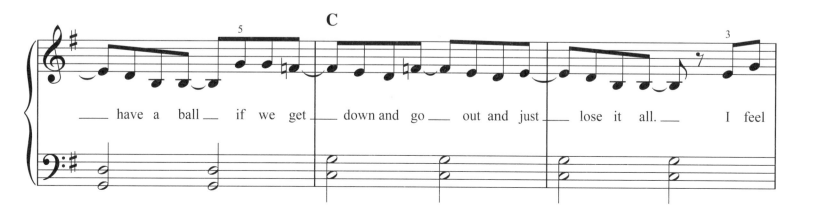

stressed _ out. I wan - na let go. Let's go way ____ out, spaced _ out and los-

ing all con - trol.

CODA

And then we'll do it a - gain. _

____ Let's do it, let's do it, let's do it, let's do it, ____ and do it, and

do it. Let's live it up, and do it, and do it, and do it, do it, do it. Let's

do it. Let's do it. Let's do it, 'cause I got-ta feel - ing

that to - night's ___ gon - na be ___ a good ___ night, ___ that to - night's ___

___ gon - na be ___ a good ___ night, that to - night's ___ gon - na be ___ a good, ___

___ good night. ___ (Woo - hoo.)

GIRLS JUST WANT TO HAVE FUN

Words and Music by
ROBERT HAZARD

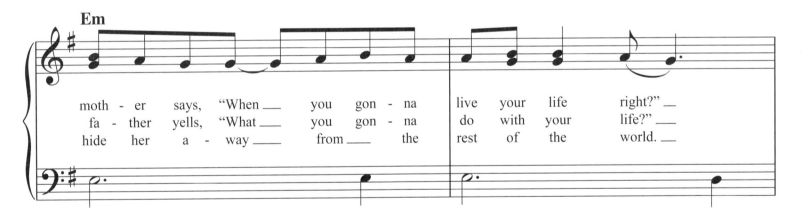

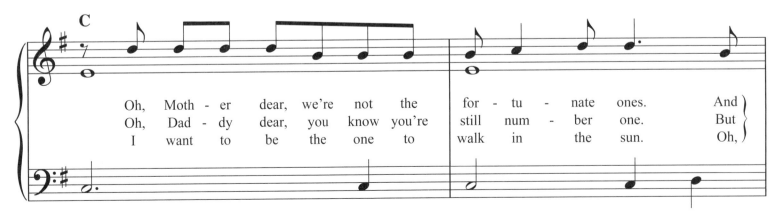

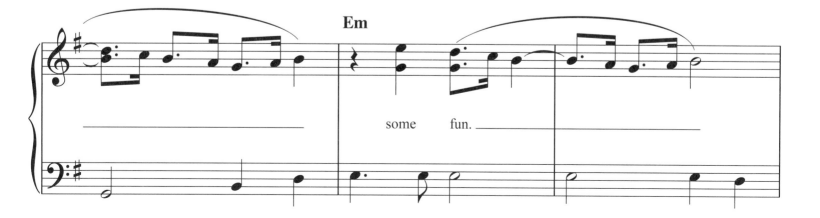

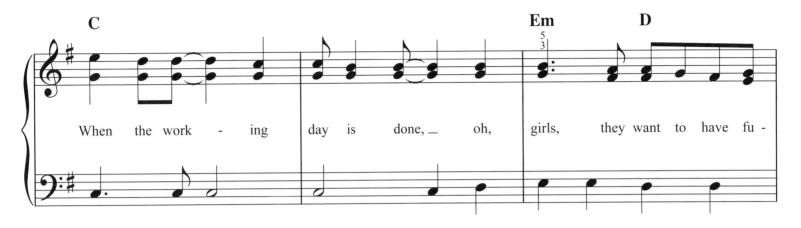

When the work - ing day is done, — oh, girls, they want to have fu -

un. Oh, _____ girls just want to have fun. _____

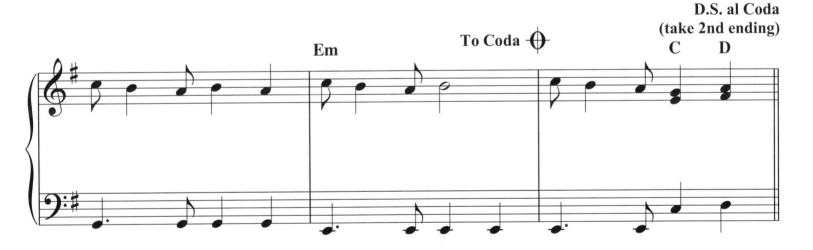

They just wan - na, they

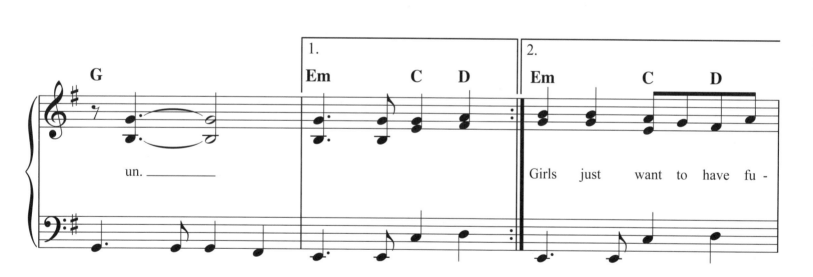

HELLO

Words and Music by ADELE ADKINS
and GREG KURSTIN

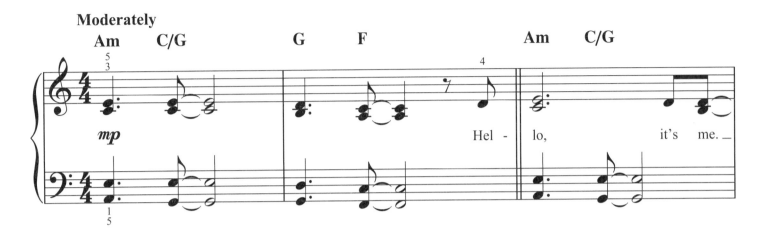

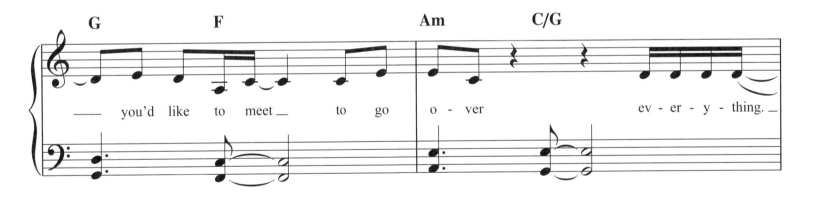

49

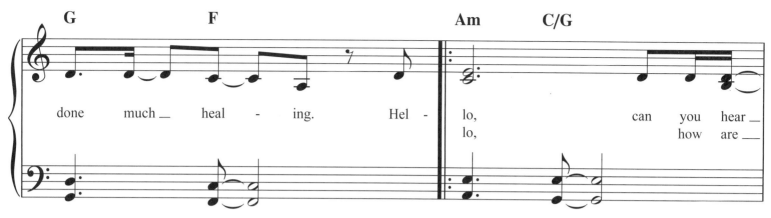

done much __ heal __ - ing. Hel -
lo,

can you hear __ how are __

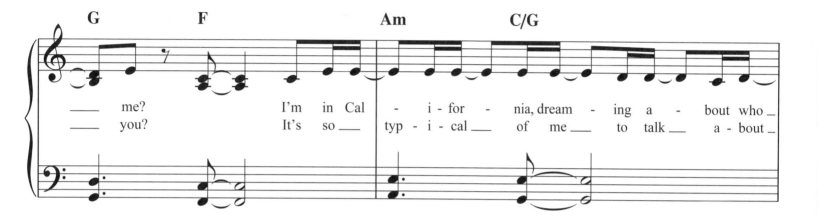

__ me? I'm in Cal - i - for - nia, dream - ing a - bout who __
__ you? It's so __ typ - i - cal __ of me __ to talk __ a - bout __

__ we used to be __ when we were young - er and free.
__ my - self; I'm sor - ry. __ I hope __ that you're

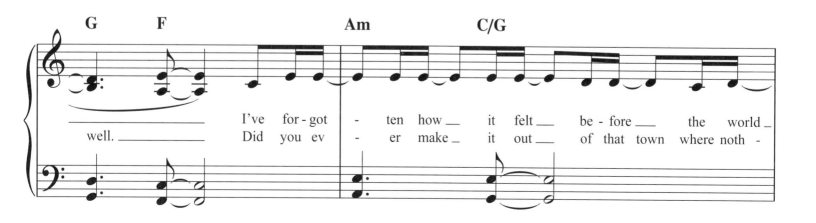

well. _____ I've for - got - ten how __ it felt __ be - fore __ the world __
Did you ev - er make __ it out __ of that town where noth -

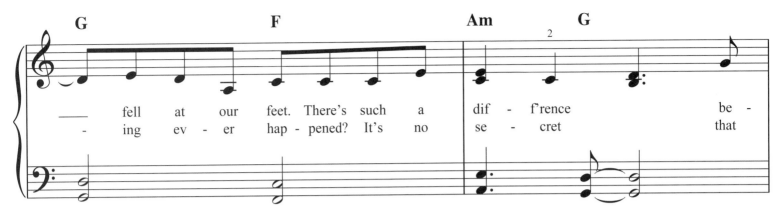

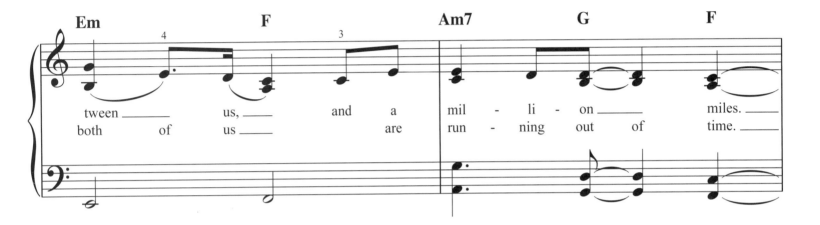

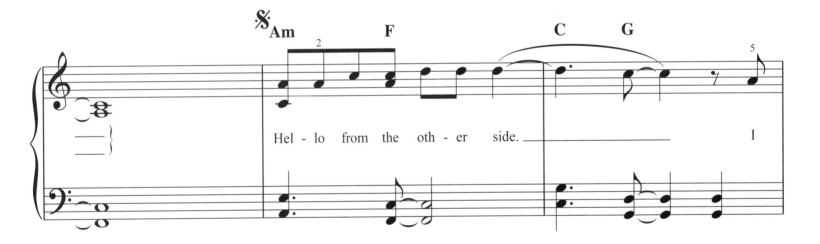

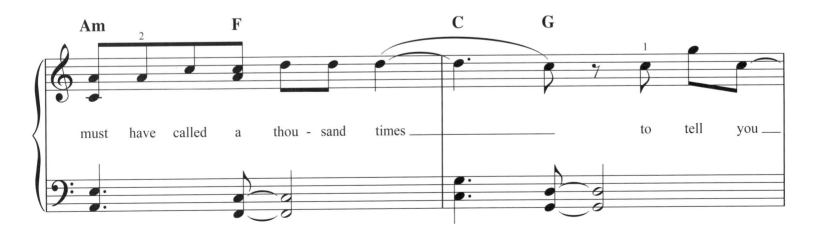

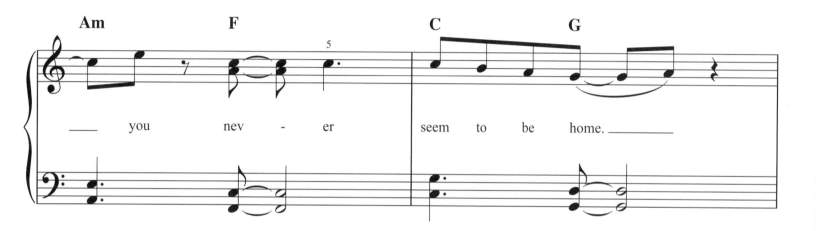

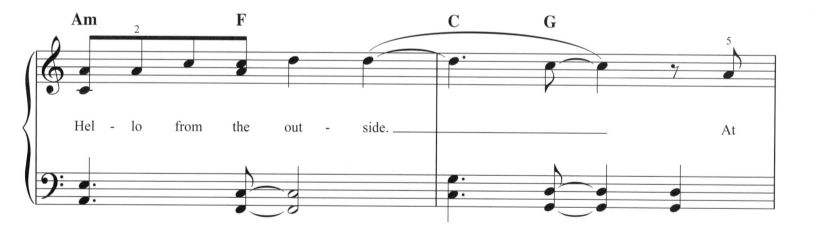

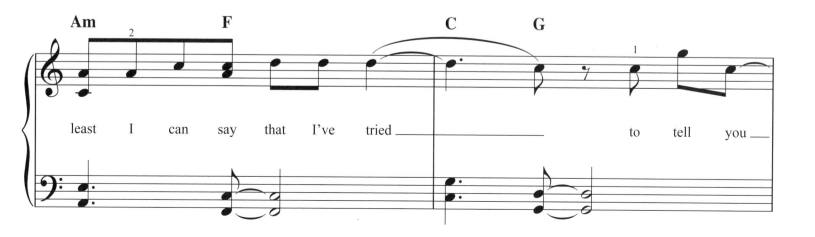

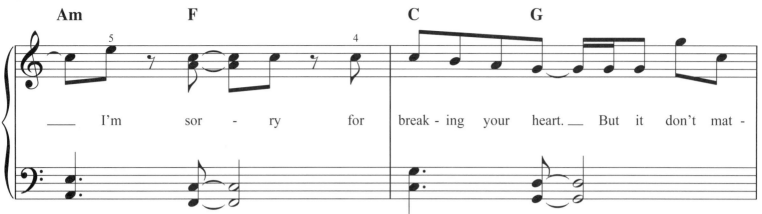

I'm sor - ry for break - ing your heart. __ But it don't mat -

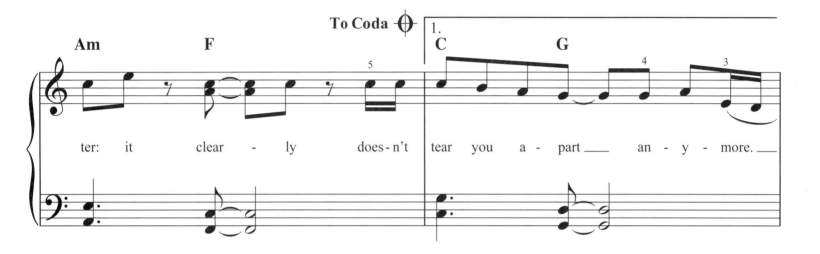

To Coda ⊕

ter: it clear - ly does-n't tear you a - part ____ an - y - more. __

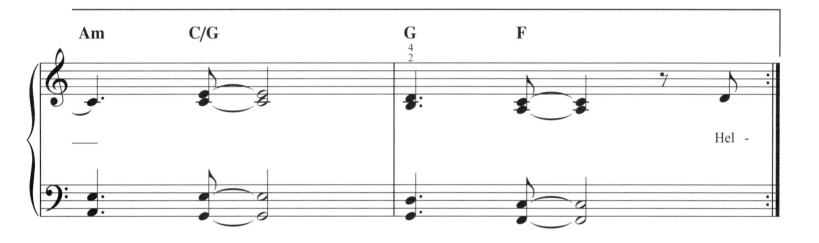

__ Hel -

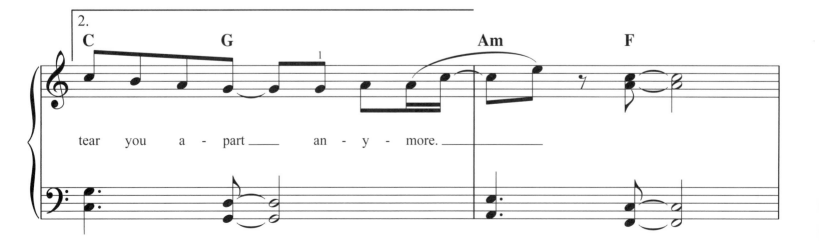

tear you a - part ____ an - y - more. __

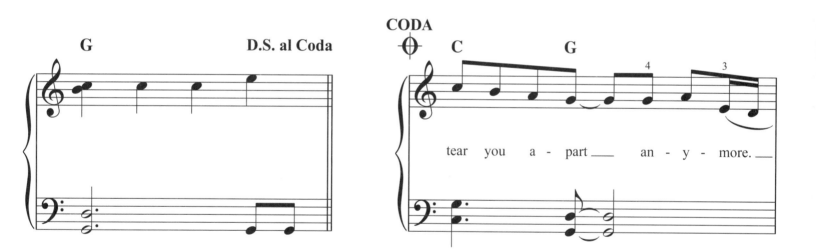

tear you a - part___ an - y - more.___

LIVIN' ON A PRAYER

Words and Music by JON BON JOVI,
DESMOND CHILD and RICHIE SAMBORA

Moderate Rock

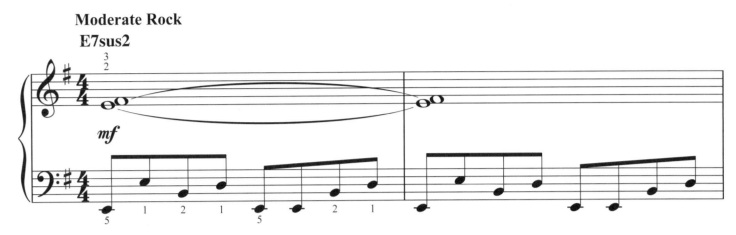

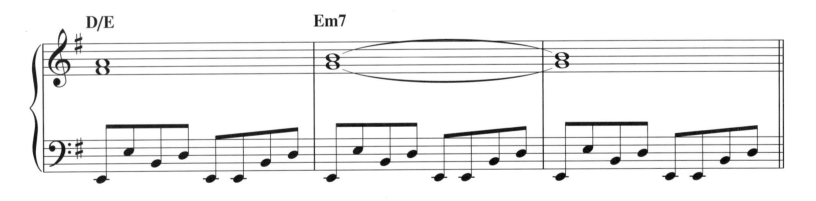

(Spoken:) Once upon a time, not so long ago...

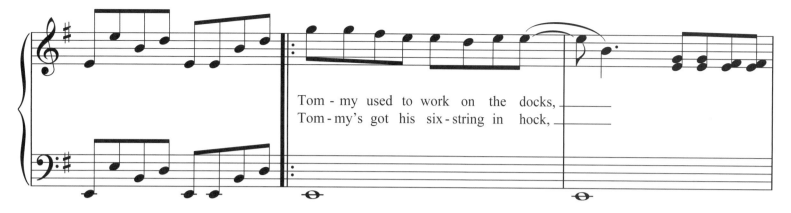

Tom - my used to work on the docks, _____
Tom - my's got his six - string in hock, _____

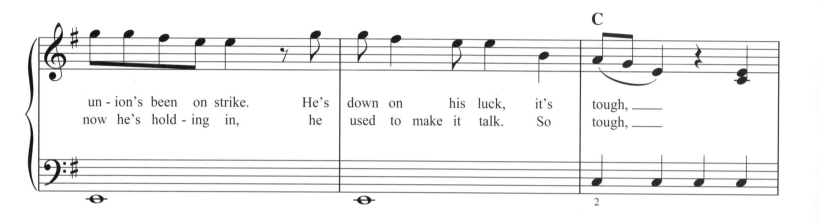

C

un - ion's been on strike. He's down on his luck, it's tough, _____
now he's hold - ing in, he used to make it talk. So tough, _____

D **Em7**

so tough. _____
it's tough. _____

Gi - na works the din - er all day, _____ work - ing for her man. She
Gi - na dreams of run - ning a - way; _____ when she cries in the night, Tom - my

brings home her pay, for love, _____ for love. __
whis - pers, "Ba - by, it's o - kay __ some - day." __

She says we've got to hold on ___ } to
We've got to hold on ___ }

what we've got. It does - n't make a dif - f'rence if we make it or not. We've

got each oth - er and that's a lot for ___ love. __ We'll

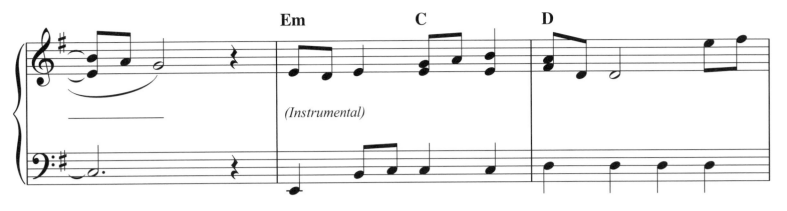

Em   C   D

(Instrumental)

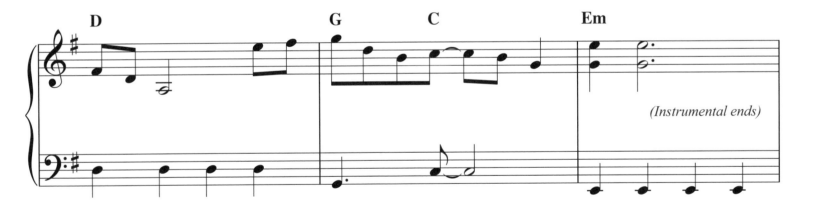

G   C   D   Em   C

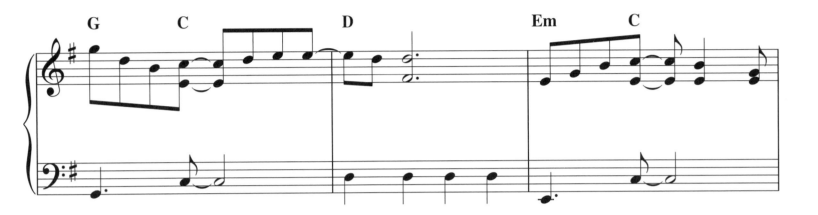

D   G   C   Em

(Instrumental ends)

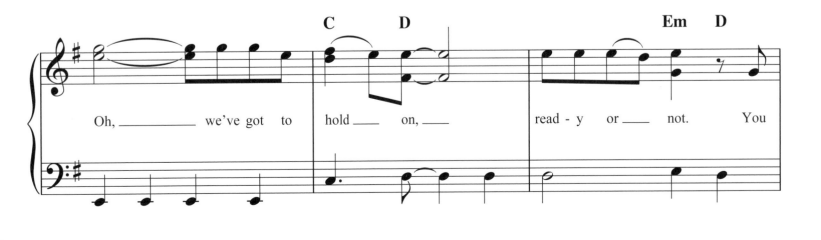

C   D   Em   D

Oh, _____ we've got to hold ___ on, ___ read - y or ___ not.   You

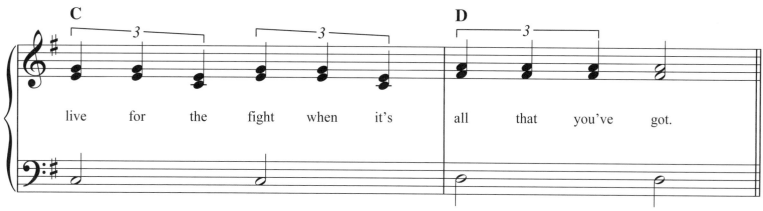

live for the fight when it's all that you've got.

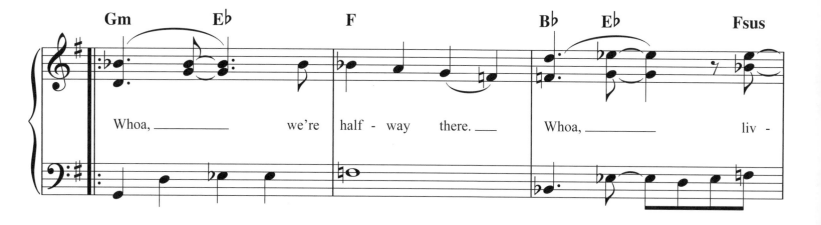

Whoa, _____ we're half - way there. ___ Whoa, _____ liv -

- in' on a prayer. ___ Take my hand, __ and we'll make it, I swear. ___

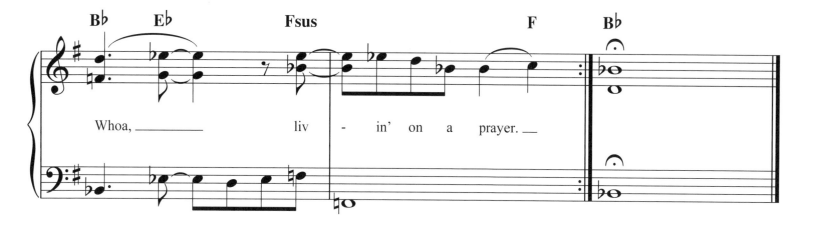

Whoa, _____ liv - in' on a prayer. ___

MACARENA

Words and Music by ANTONIO ROMERO
and RAFAEL RUIZ

Da - le a tu cuer-po a - le - grí - a Ma - ca - re - na que tu

cuer - po es pá dar - le a - le - gri - a y co - sa bue - na. Da - le a tu cuer - po a - le -

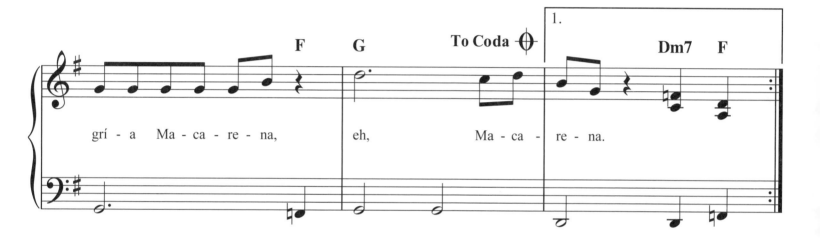

grí - a Ma - ca - re - na, eh, Ma - ca - re - na.

re - na. Ma - ca - re - na tie - ne un no - vio que se lla - ma, que se

lla - ma, de a - pe - lli - do Vi - to - ri - no. Y en la ju - ra de ban - de - ra del mu -

cha - cho se la dió con dos a - mi - gos. Ma - ca -

re - na tie - ne un no - vio que se lla - ma, que se

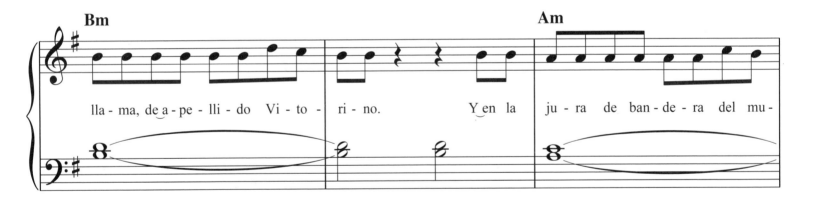

lla - ma, de a - pe - lli - do Vi - to - ri - no. Y en la ju - ra de ban - de - ra del mu -

D.S. al Coda

cha - cho se la dió con dos a - mi - gos.

CODA

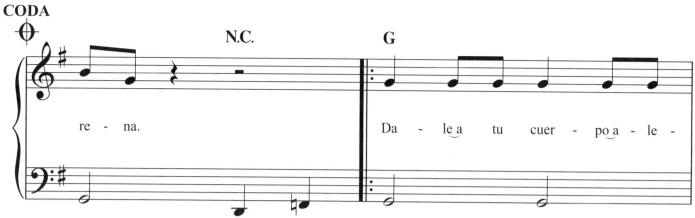

re - na.

Da - le a tu cuer - po a - le -

grí - a Ma - ca - re - na que tu cuer - po es pá dar - le a - le - gri - a y co - sa bue - na.

Da - le a tu cuer - po a - le - grí - a Ma - ca - re - na, eh, Ma - ca -

re - na. eh, Ma - ca - re - na.

MR. BRIGHTSIDE

Words and Music by BRANDON FLOWERS,
DAVE KEUNING, MARK STOERMER
and RONNIE VANNUCCI

Quickly, with a beat

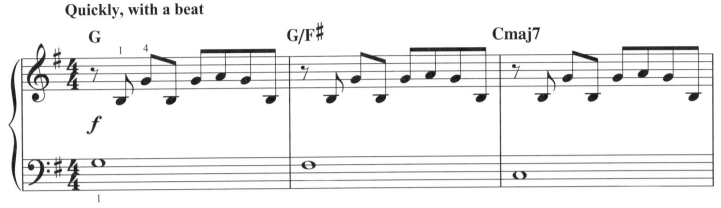

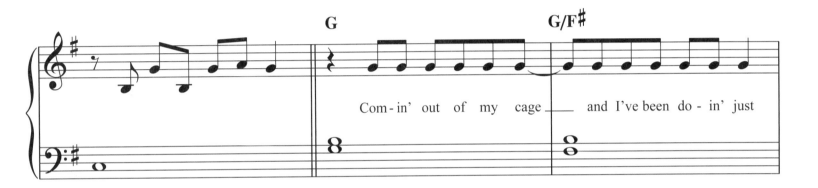

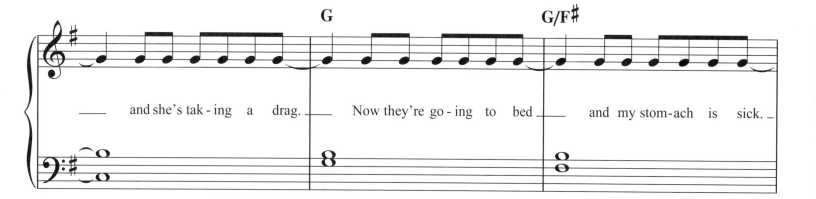

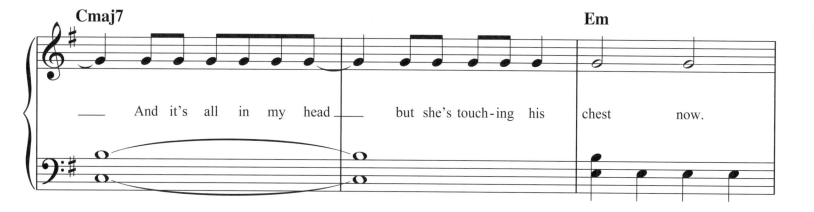

I just can't look. It's kill - ing me _____ and

tak - ing con - trol.

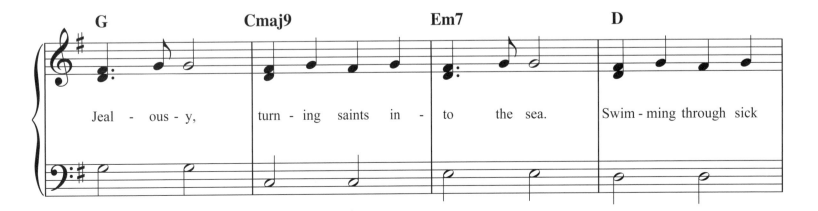

Jeal - ous - y, turn - ing saints in - to the sea. Swim - ming through sick

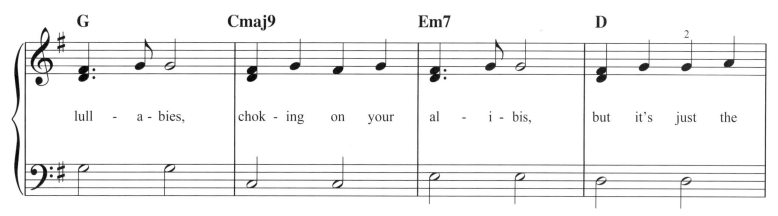

lull - a - bies, chok - ing on your al - i - bis, but it's just the

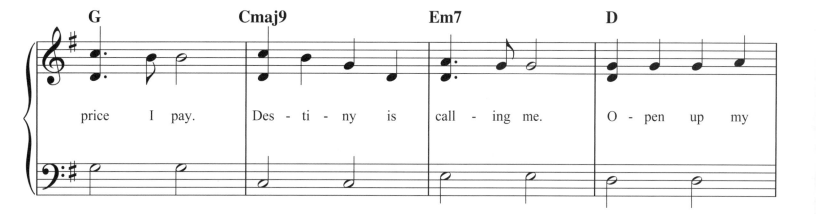

price I pay. Des - ti - ny is call - ing me. O - pen up my

ea - ger eyes _____ 'cause I'm Mis - ter Bright - side.

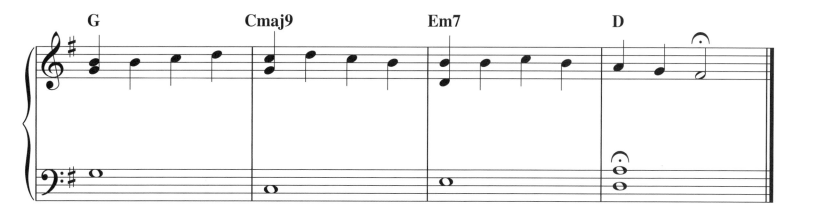

OLD TOWN ROAD
(Remix)

Words and Music by TRENT REZNOR,
BILLY RAY CYRUS, JOCELYN DONALD,
ATTICUS ROSS, KIOWA ROUKEMA
and MONTERO LAMAR HILL

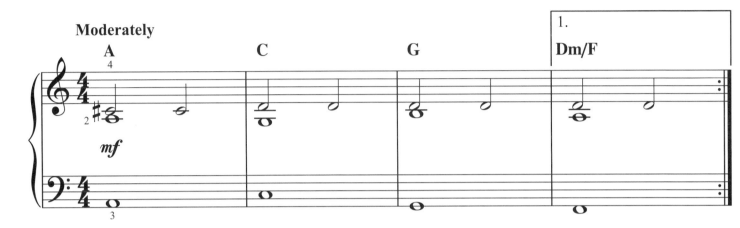

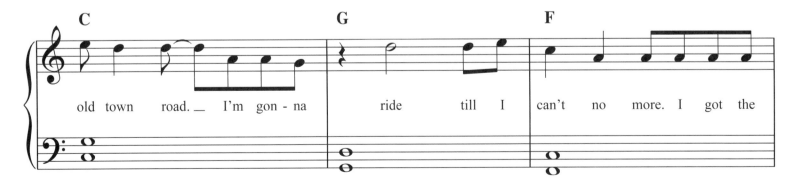

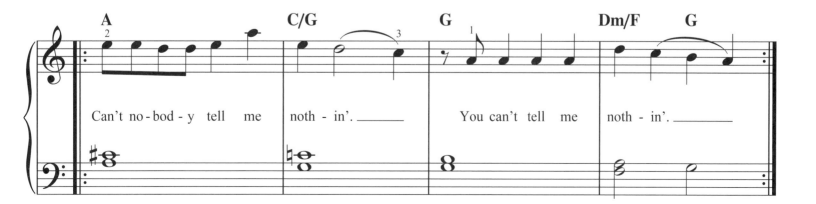

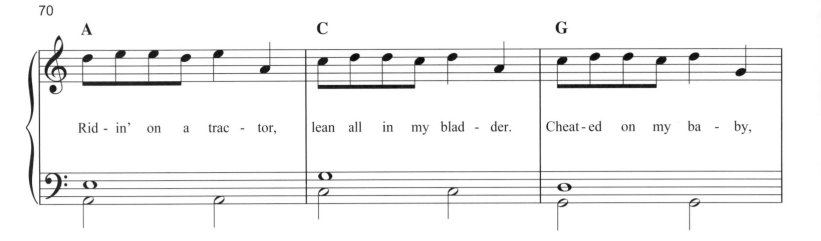

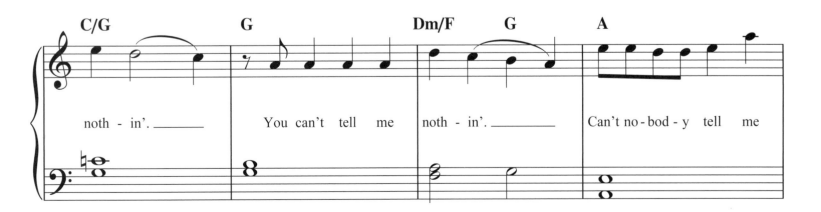

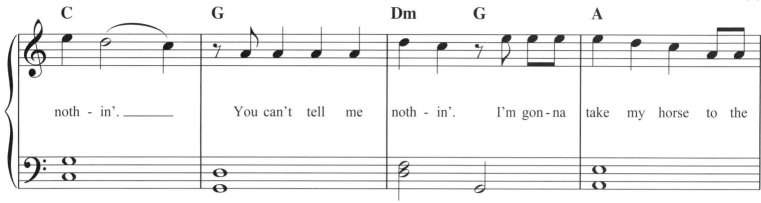

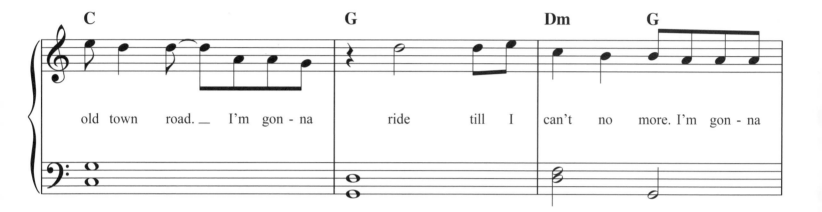

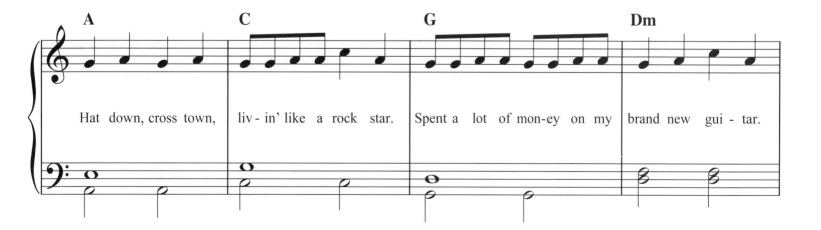

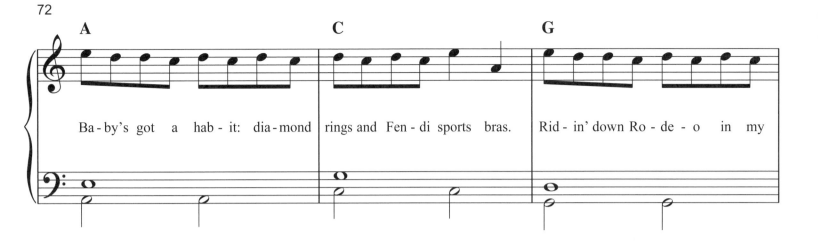

Ba - by's got a hab - it: dia - mond rings and Fen - di sports bras.
Rid - in' down Ro - de - o in my

Ma - se - ra - ti sports car. Got no stress; I've been through all that. __ I'm like a

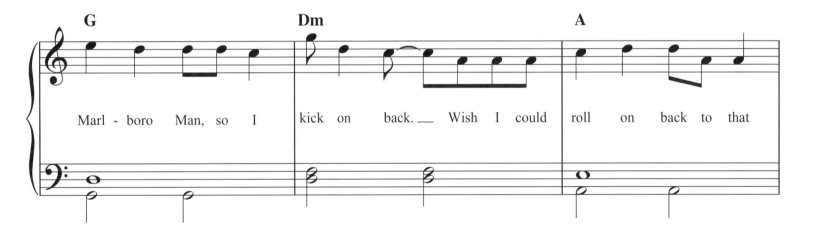

Marl - boro Man, so I kick on back. __ Wish I could roll on back to that

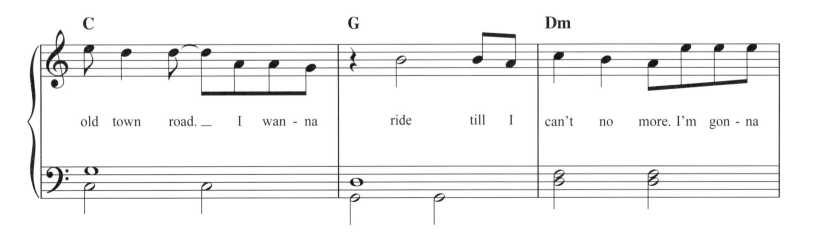

old town road. __ I wan - na ride till I can't no more. I'm gon - na

take my horse to the | old town road. __ I'm gon-na | ride till I can't no more. I'm gon-na

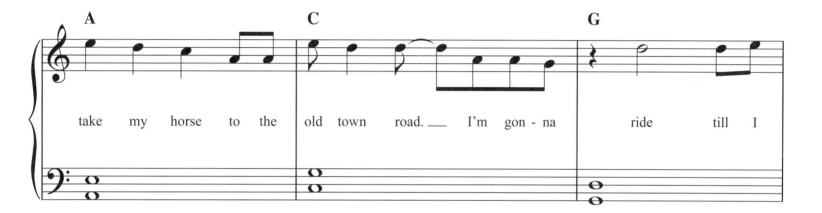

take my horse to the | old town road. __ I'm gon - na | ride till I

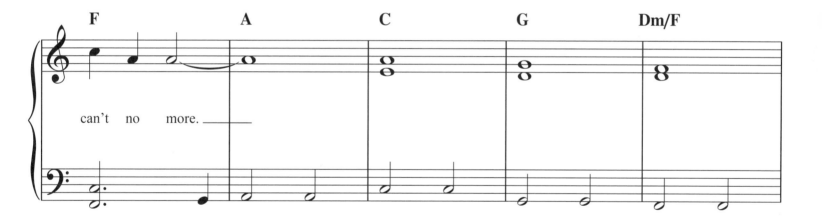

can't no more. __

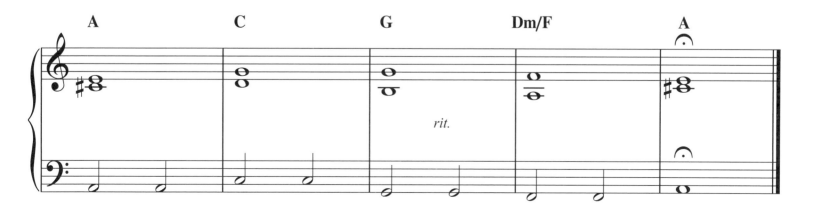

rit.

ONE DANCE

Words and Music by AUBREY GRAHAM,
AYODEJI BALOGUN, ERROL REID,
PAUL JEFFRIES, NOAH SHEBIB,
KYLA REID, COREY JOHNSON
and LUKE REID

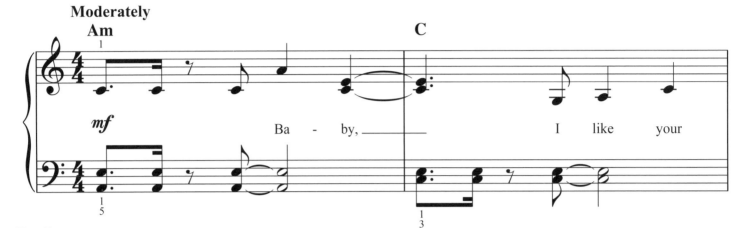

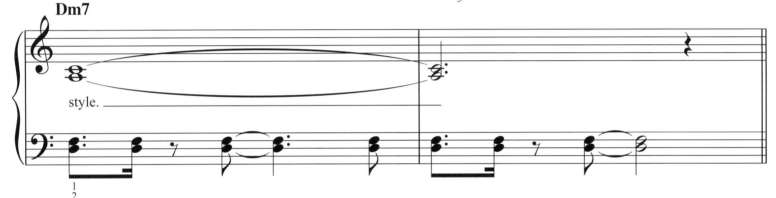

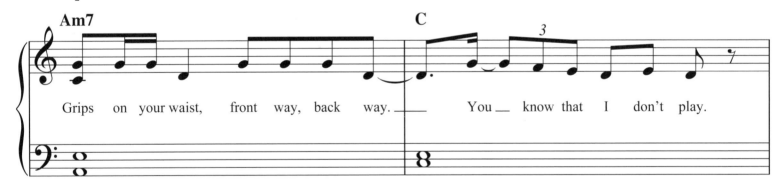

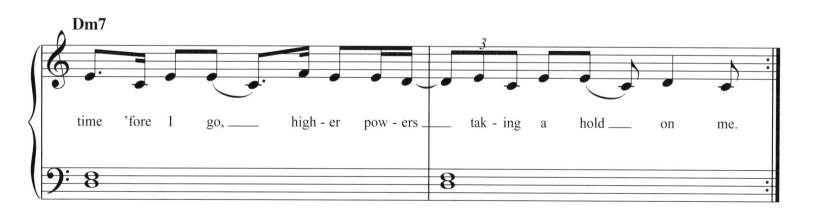

76

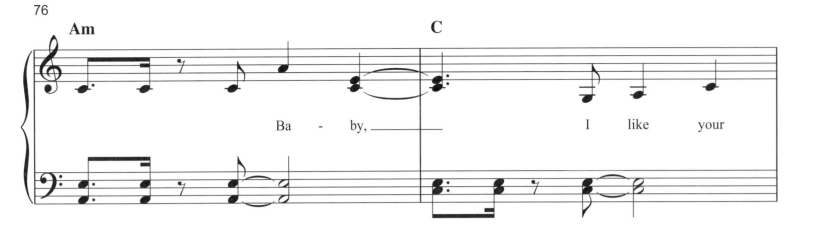

Ba - by, _____ I like your

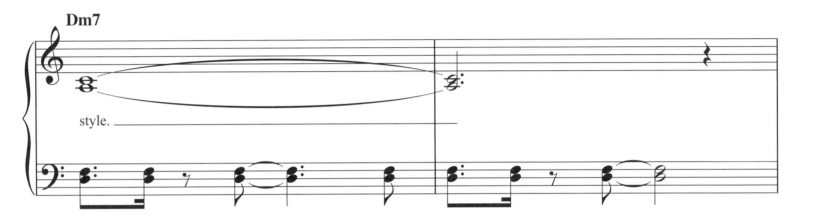

style. _____

Strength and guid-ance ___ all that I'm wish-ing for my friends. __ No - bod - y

makes it from my ends. ___ I had to bust up the si - lence. __ You know

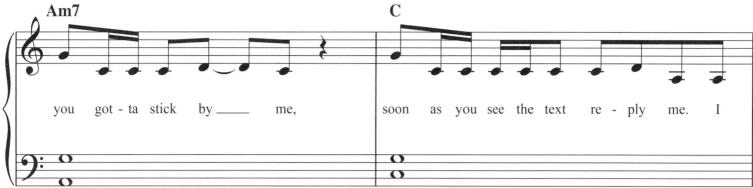

you got-ta stick by ____ me, soon as you see the text re-ply me. I

don't wan-na spend time fight-ing. We've __ got no ____ time and that's why

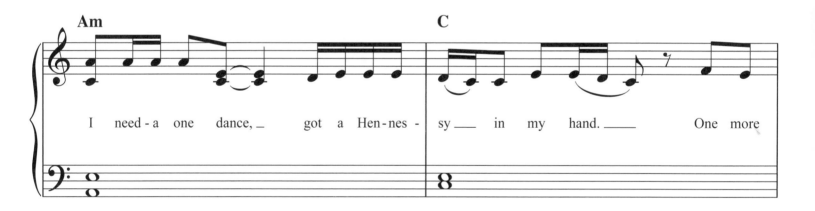

I need-a one dance, __ got a Hen-nes-sy __ in my hand. ____ One more

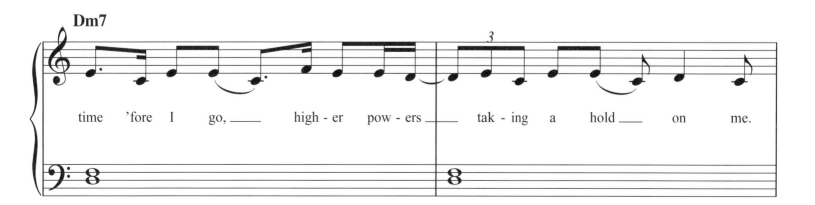

time 'fore I go, ____ high-er pow-ers ____ tak-ing a hold ____ on me.

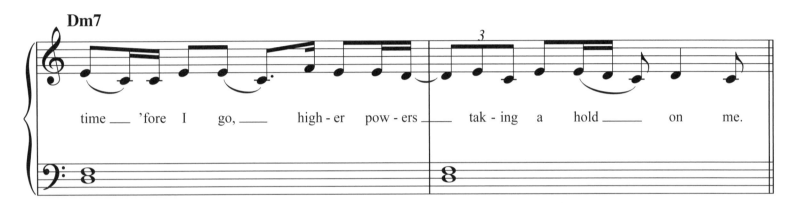

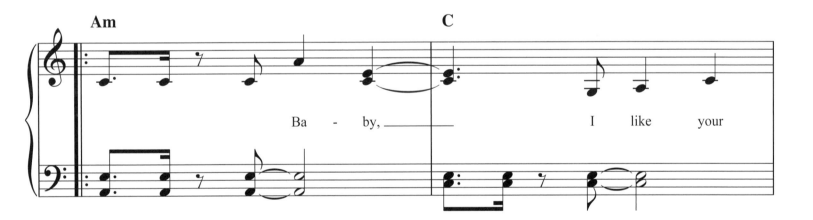

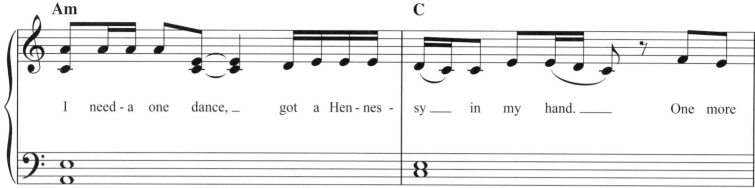

I need-a one dance, ___ got a Hen-nes - sy ___ in my hand. ___ One more

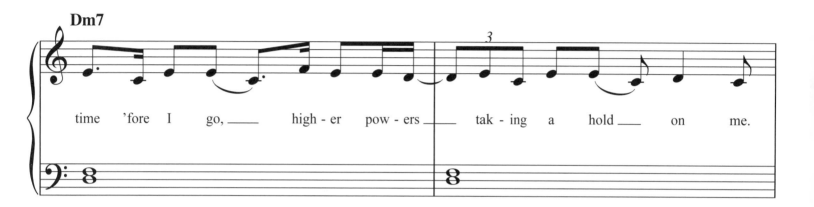

time 'fore I go, ___ high - er pow-ers ___ tak - ing a hold ___ on me.

I need-a one dance, ___ got a Hen-nes - sy ___ in my hand. ___ One more

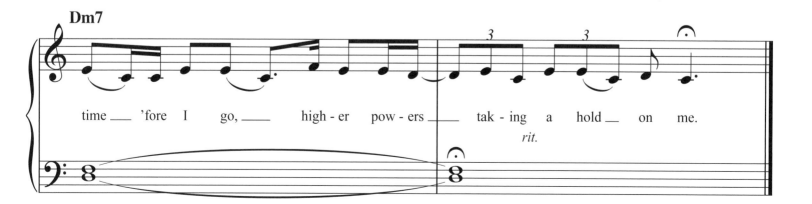

time ___ 'fore I go, ___ high - er pow-ers ___ tak - ing a hold ___ on me.

100 YEARS

Words and Music by
JOHN ONDRASIK

Moderately fast

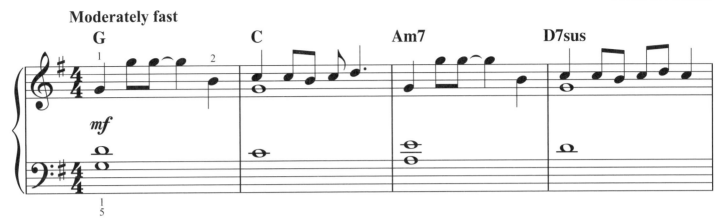

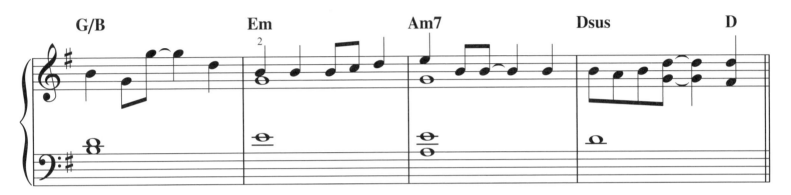

I'm fif - teen ____ for a mo - ment,
I'm twen - ty-two for a mo - ment,

caught in ____ be -
and she ____ feels

tween ten and twen - ty and
bet - ter than ev - er and

I'm just dream -
we're on fire, ____

ing,
count - ing the
mak - ing our

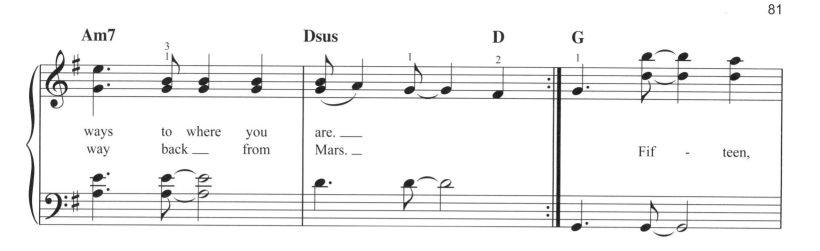

ways   to where   you   are. ___
way   back ___ from   Mars. ___
Fif   -   teen,

there's still   time ___ for   you.   Time ____ to   buy and   time ___ to   lose. _

___   Fif   -   teen, ____   there's nev - er   a   wish   bet - ter than

this   when you   on - ly got ___ a   hun - dred years   to

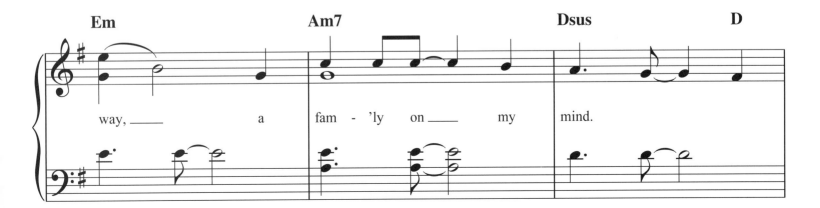

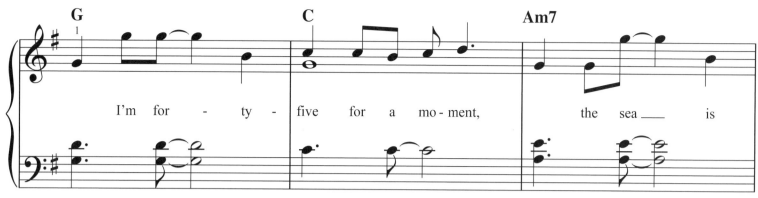

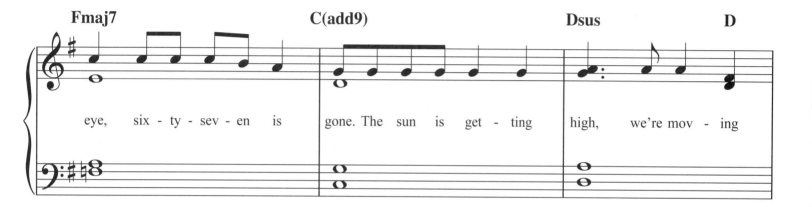

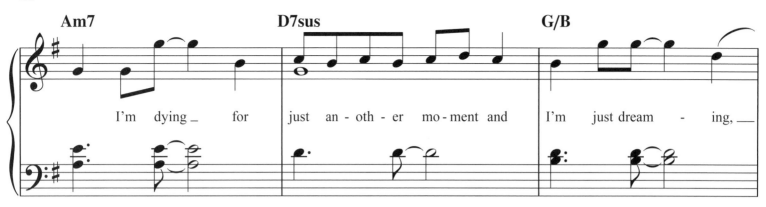

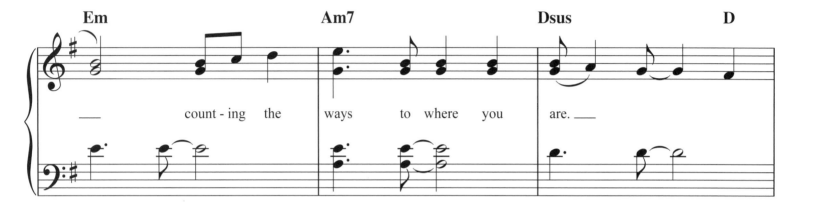

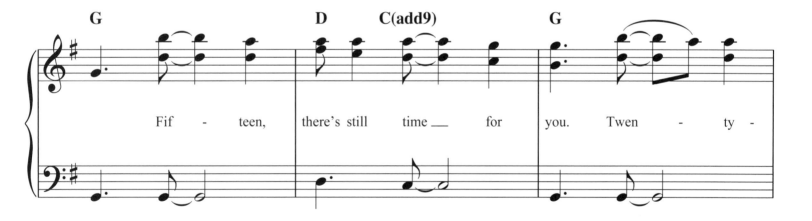

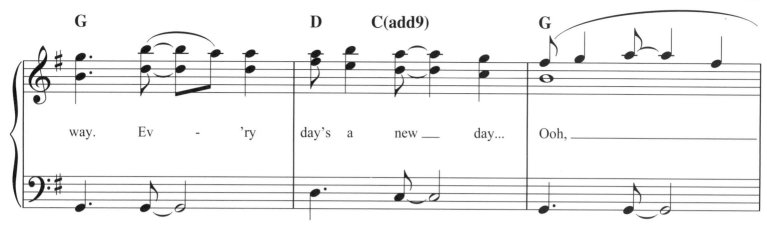

way. Ev - 'ry day's a new __ day... Ooh, _____

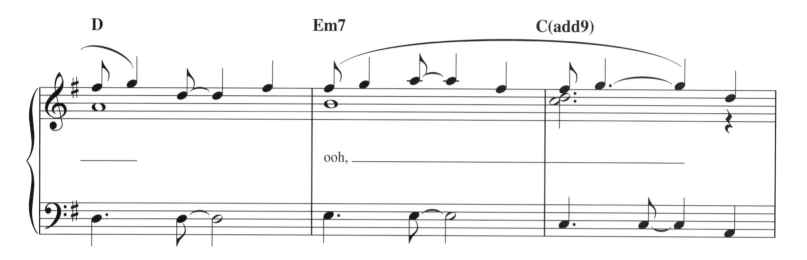

__ ooh, _____

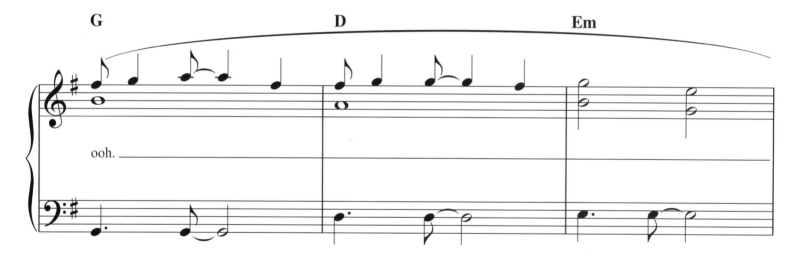

ooh. _____

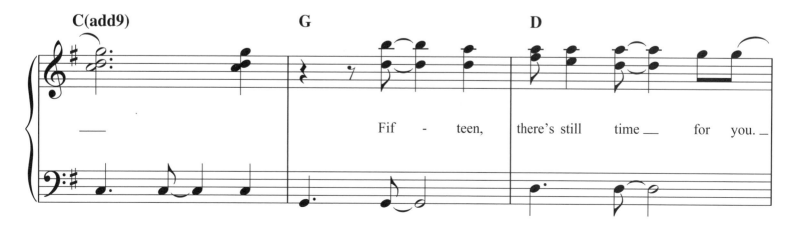

__ Fif - teen, there's still time __ for you. __

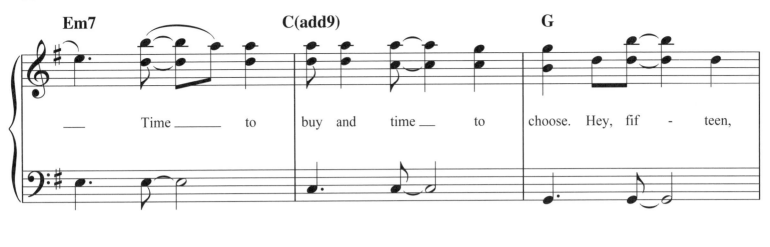

Time ___ to buy and time __ to choose. Hey, fif - teen,

there's nev - er a wish bet - ter than this when you

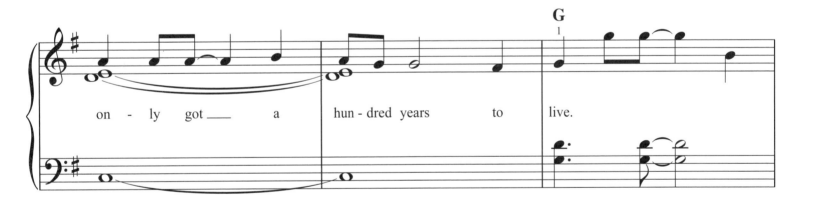

on - ly got ___ a hun - dred years to live.

rit.

SHAKE IT OFF

Words and Music by TAYLOR SWIFT,
MAX MARTIN and SHELLBACK

Moderately fast

N.C.

I stay out too late, got noth-ing in my brain;
beat; I'm light-ning on my feet.

that's what peo - ple say, _____ mm, mm. That's what peo-ple
And that's what they don't see, _____ mm, mm. That's what they don't

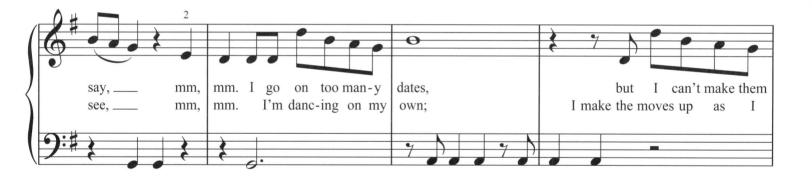

say, ____ mm, mm. I go on too man-y dates, but I can't make them
see, ____ mm, mm. I'm danc-ing on my own; I make the moves up as I

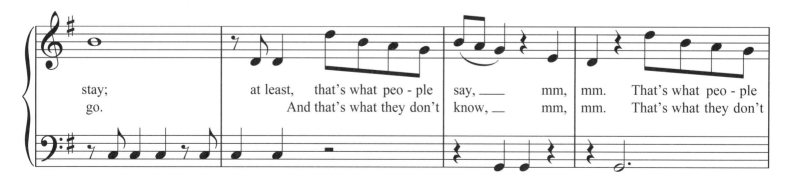

stay; at least, that's what peo - ple say, ____ mm, mm. That's what peo - ple
go. And that's what they don't know, __ mm, mm. That's what they don't

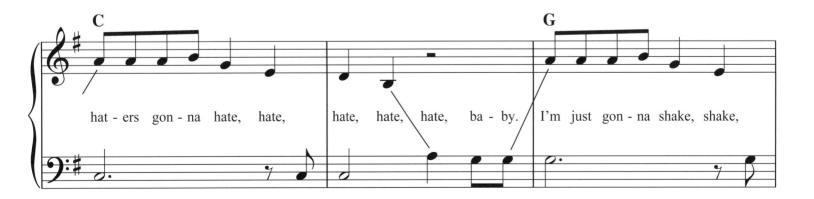

shake, shake, shake; _ I shake it off, I shake it off. (Ooh, _ ooh!) Heart -

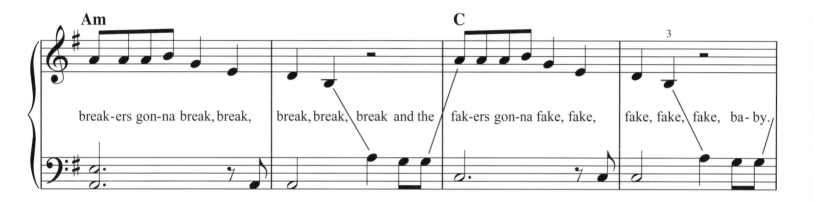

break-ers gon-na break, break, break, break, break and the fak-ers gon-na fake, fake, fake, fake, fake, ba- by.

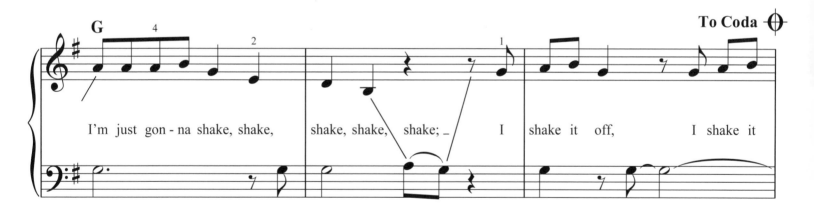

I'm just gon - na shake, shake, shake, shake, shake; _ I shake it off, I shake it

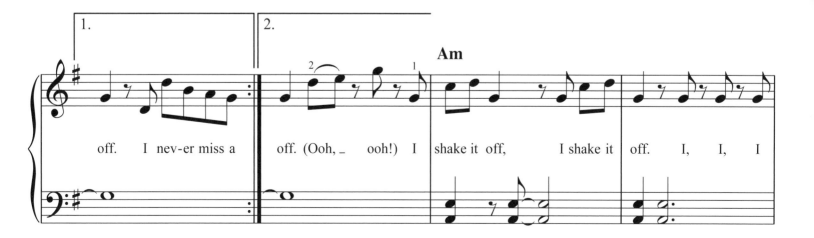

1.
off. I nev-er miss a

2.
off. (Ooh, _ ooh!) I shake it off, I shake it off. I, I, I

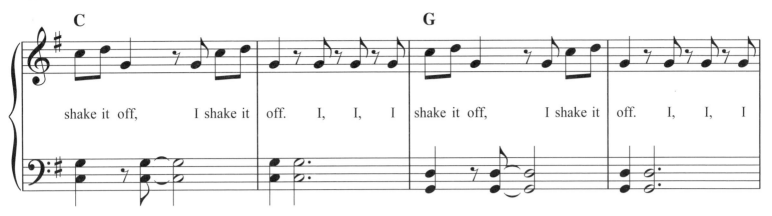

shake it off,   I shake it   off.   I,   I,   I   shake it off,   I shake it   off.   I,   I,   I

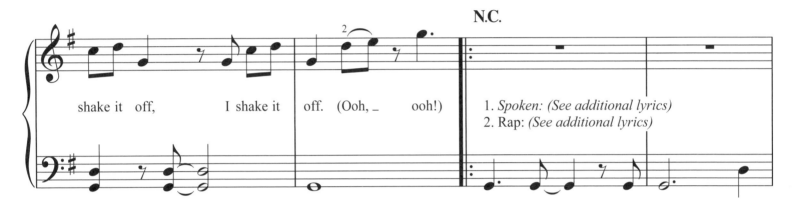

shake it off,   I shake it   off. (Ooh, _ ooh!)   1. *Spoken: (See additional lyrics)*
2. Rap: *(See additional lyrics)*

D.S. al Coda

Rap ends   Yeah, _   oh. _____ 'Cause the

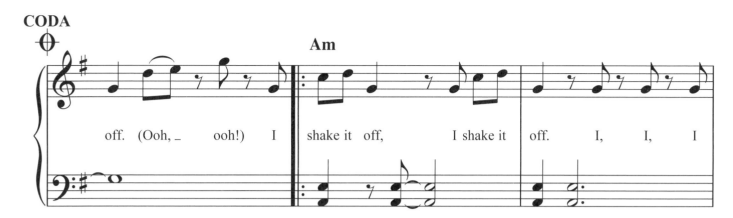

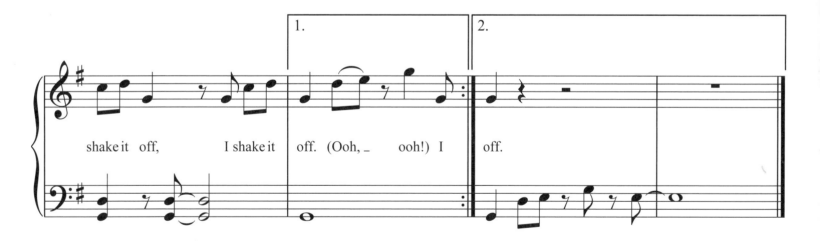

Additional Lyrics

Spoken: Hey, hey, hey! Just think: While you've been getting
Down and out about the liars and the dirty, dirty
Cheats of the world, you could've been getting down to
This. Sick. Beat!

Rap: My ex-man brought his new girlfriend.
She's like, "Oh, my god!" But I'm just gonna shake.
And to the fella over there with the hella good hair,
Won't you come on over, baby? We can shake, shake, shake.

ROCKET MAN
(I Think It's Gonna Be a Long Long Time)

Words and Music by ELTON JOHN
and BERNIE TAUPIN

Moderately, in 2

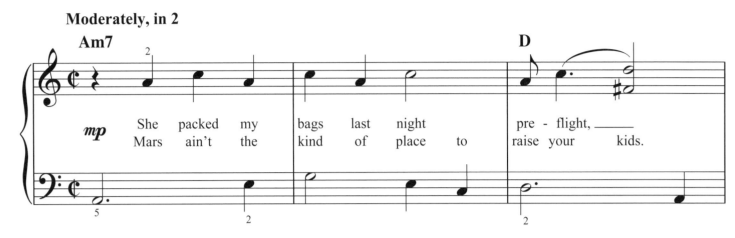

She packed my bags last night pre-flight, _____
Mars ain't the kind of place to raise your kids.

ze-ro ho-ur, nine A. M.
In fact, it's cold as hell.

And I'm gon-na be high _____
And there's no one _____ there to

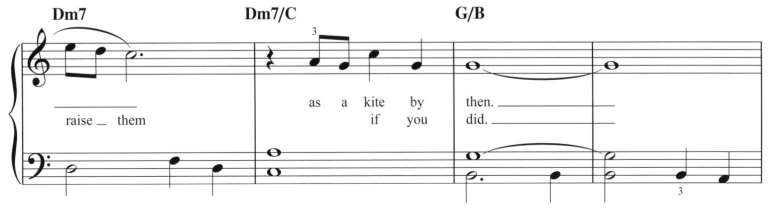

raise ___ them
as a kite by then. _____
if you did. _____

G · · · · **Am7**

I miss the earth so much. I
And all this sci - ence, I don't

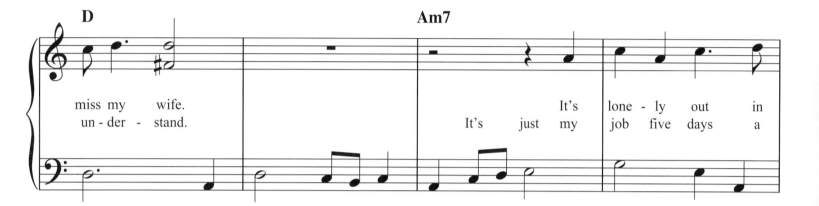

D · · · · **Am7**

miss my wife. It's lone - ly out in
un - der - stand. It's just my job five days a

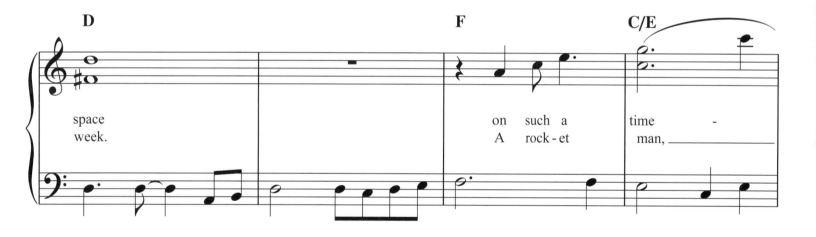

D · · · · **F** · **C/E**

space on such a time -
week. A rock - et man, _____

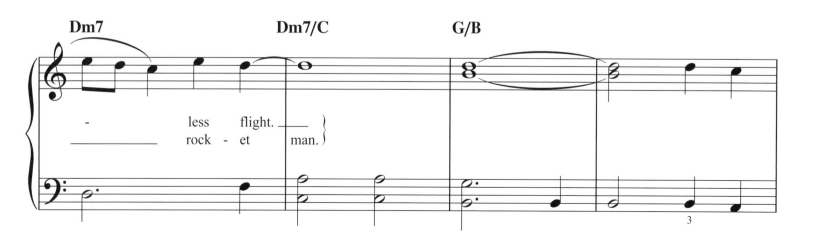

Dm7 · · · **Dm7/C** · **G/B**

- less flight. _____
_____ rock - et man.

3

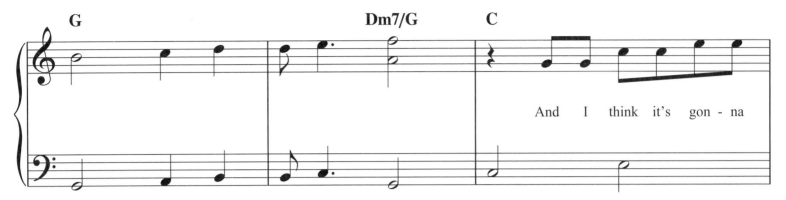

G　　　　　　　　　　　　　　**Dm7/G**　　**C**

And I think it's gon - na

　　　　　　　　　F

be a long, long time till touch-down brings me 'round a - gain to

C　　　　　　　　　　　　　　　　　　**F**

find I'm not the man they think I am at home. Oh, no, ___ no,

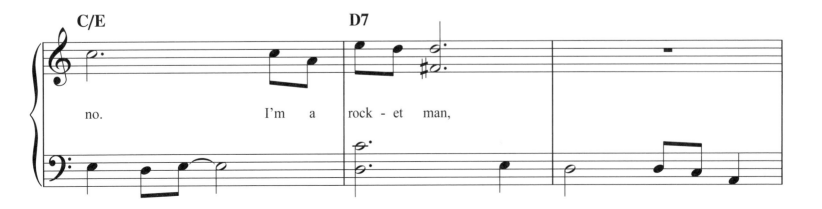

C/E　　　　　　　　**D7**

no. I'm a rock - et man,

rock - et man, burn - ing out his fuse up here a - lone.

1. **2.**

And I

think it's gon - na be a long, long time.

And I think it's gon - na be a long, long time.

SWEET CHILD O' MINE

Words and Music by W. AXL ROSE, SLASH,
IZZY STRADLIN', DUFF McKAGAN
and STEVEN ADLER

Medium Rock

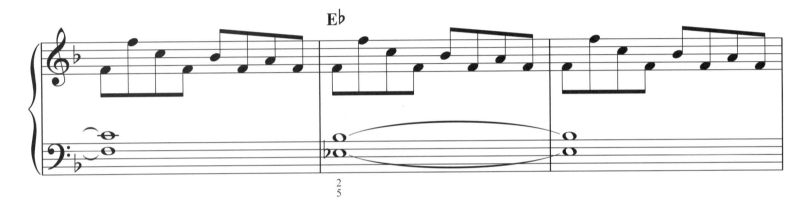

1. She's got a smile _ that it seems to me _ re - minds me of child - hood
2. *(See additional lyrics)*

mem - o - ries, ___ where ev - 'ry - thing ___ was as fresh ___ as the bright ___ blue

sky. _____

Now and then ___ when I

see her face ___ she takes me a - way ___ to that spe - cial place, ___ and if I

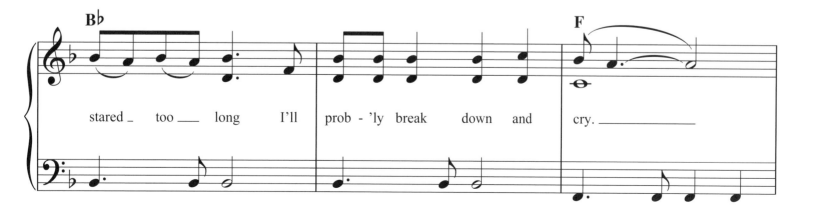

stared ___ too ___ long I'll prob - 'ly break down and cry. _____

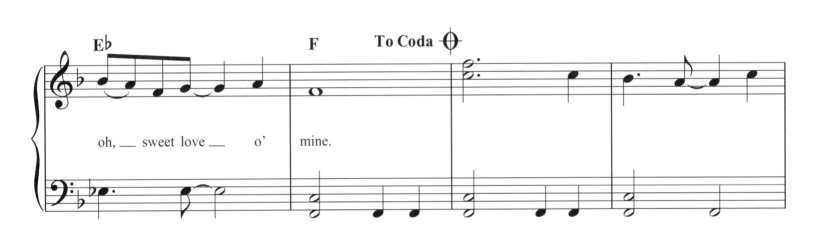

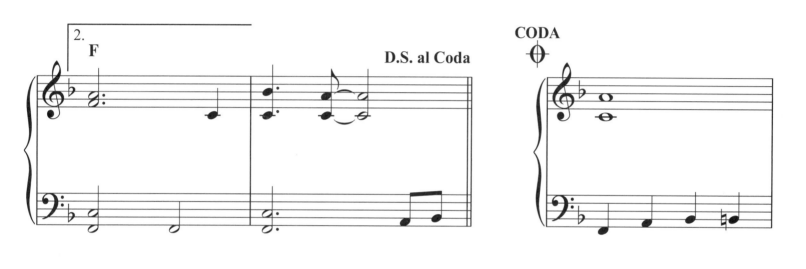

Oh, oh, ___ oh, oh, ___ sweet child ___ o' mine. ___

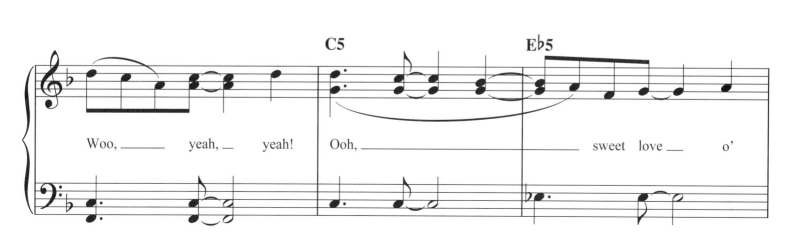

Woo, ___ yeah, ___ yeah! Ooh, ___ sweet love ___ o'

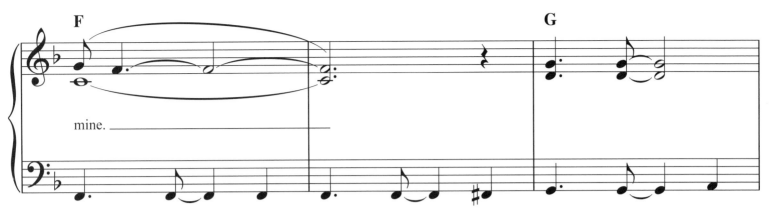

Where do we go ___ now? No, no, no, no, no, no, no. Sweet

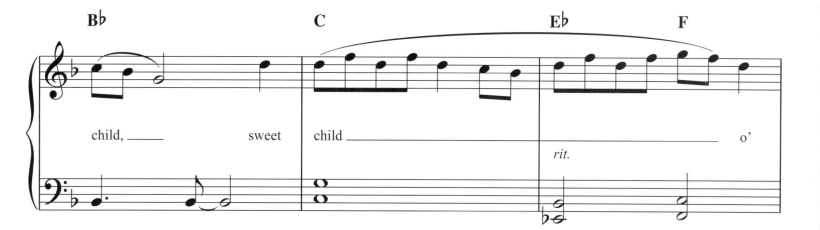

child, _____ sweet child _____ o'

rit.

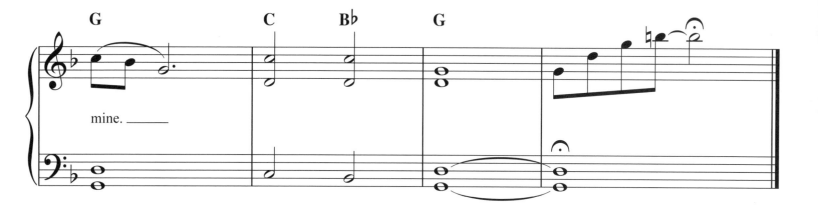

mine. _____

Additional Lyrics

2. She's got eyes of the bluest skies, as if they thought of rain.
   I hate to look into those eyes and see an ounce of pain.
   Her hair reminds me of a warm safe place where as a child I'd hide,
   And pray for the thunder and the rain to quietly pass me by.

UPTOWN FUNK

Words and Music by MARK RONSON,
BRUNO MARS, PHILIP LAWRENCE,
JEFF BHASKER, DEVON GALLASPY,
NICHOLAUS WILLIAMS, LONNIE SIMMONS,
RONNIE WILSON, CHARLES WILSON,
RUDOLPH TAYLOR and ROBERT WILSON

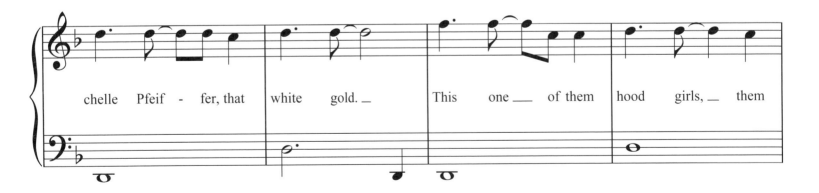

105

damn.) Make a drag - on want __ to re - tire __ man. __ I'm too

hot. (Hot damn.) Say my name, __ you know

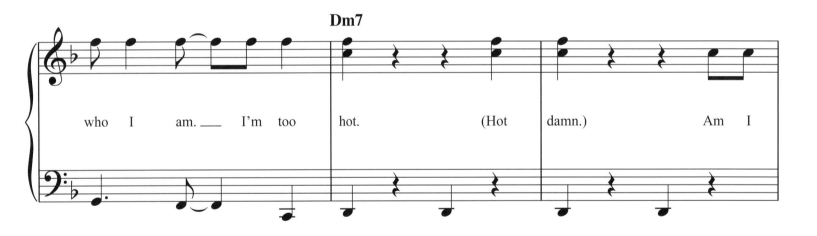

who I am. __ I'm too hot. (Hot damn.) Am I

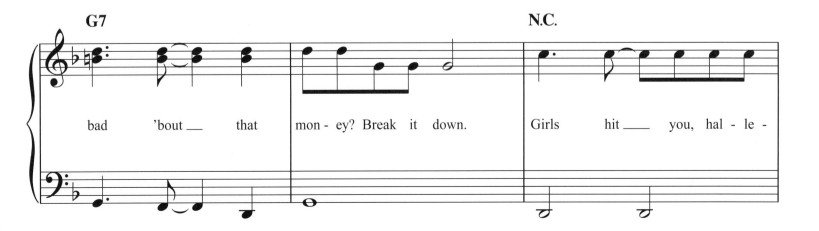

bad 'bout __ that mon - ey? Break it down. Girls hit __ you, hal - le -

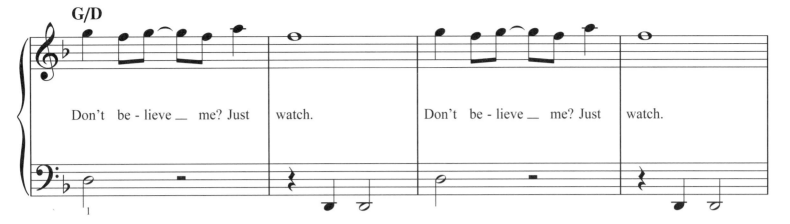

Ju - li - o,   get the stretch! Ride to Har - lem,   Hol - ly - wood,

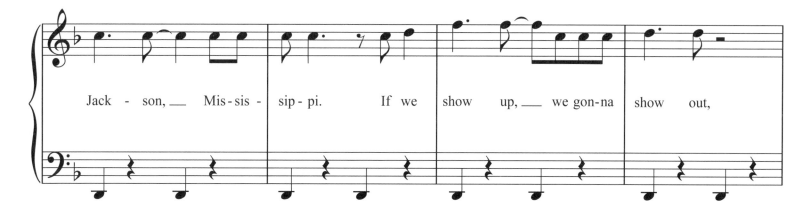

Jack - son, ___ Mis - sis - sip - pi.   If we   show   up, ___ we gon-na   show   out,

D.S. al Coda

CODA

G7/D

smooth-er than a fresh jar of Skip-py.   I'm too

Hey, hey,   hey, ___ oh!

Dm

G7

1.

Up - town   funk you up. ___

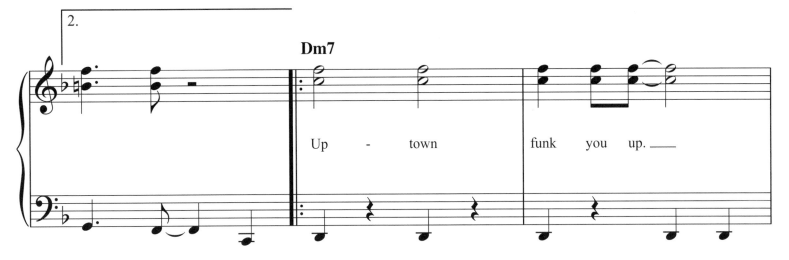

2.

Dm7

Up - town funk you up. ___

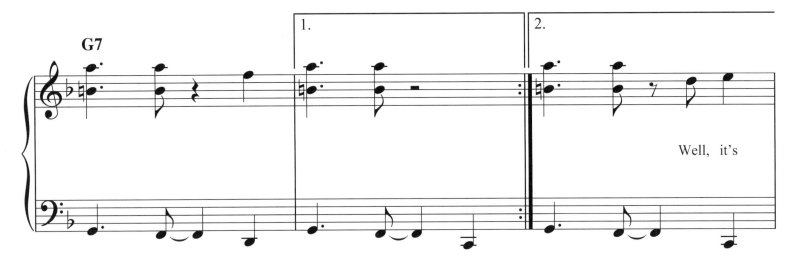

G7

1.

2.

Well, it's

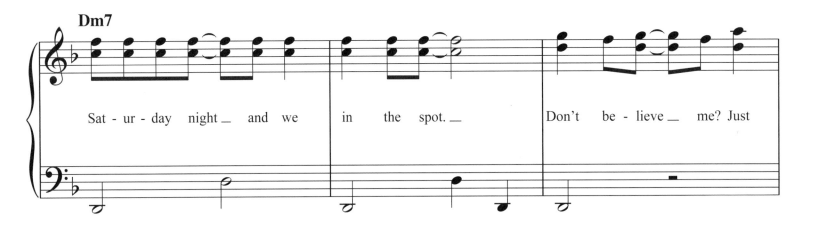

Dm7

Sat - ur - day night ___ and we in the spot. ___ Don't be - lieve ___ me? Just

Gm7/D

watch. Don't be - lieve ___ me? Just watch.

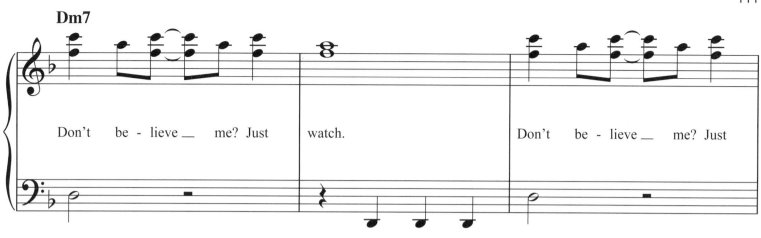

Don't be - lieve __ me? Just watch.   Don't be - lieve __ me? Just

watch.   Hey, hey, hey, _____ oh!

Up - town   funk you up. __

WE BELONG TOGETHER

Words and Music by MARIAH CAREY,
JERMAINE DUPRI, MANUEL SEAL,
JOHNTA AUSTIN, DARNELL BRISTOL,
KENNETH EDMONDS, SIDNEY JOHNSON,
PATRICK MOTEN, BOBBY WOMACK
and SANDRA SULLY

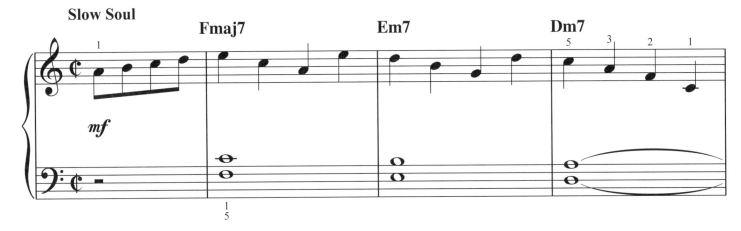

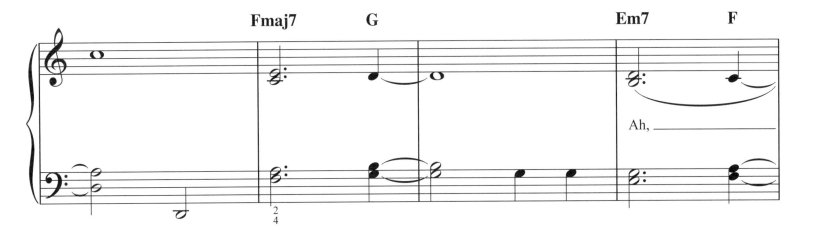

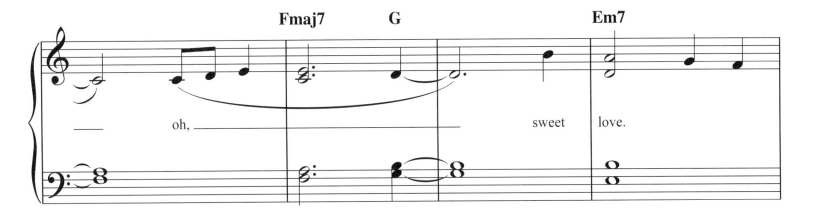

sit - ting here be - side my - self. ___

Guess I did - n't know you, guess I did - n't know

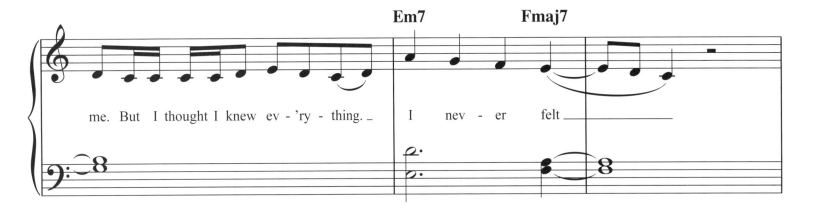

me. But I thought I knew ev - 'ry - thing. _

I nev - er felt ___

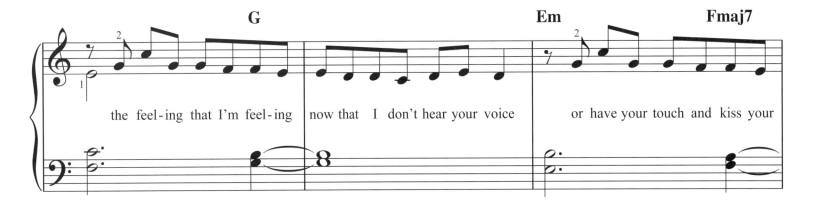

the feel - ing that I'm feel - ing

now that I don't hear your voice

or have your touch and kiss your

lips 'cause I don't have a choice.

Oh, what I would - n't give to

have you ly - ing by my side

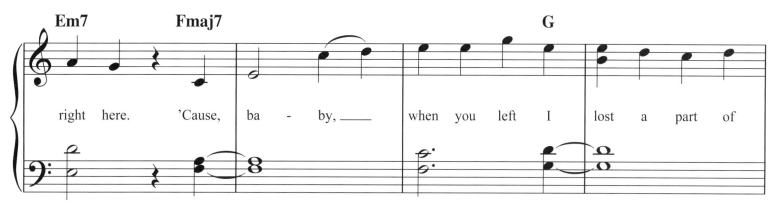

right here. 'Cause, ba - by, _____ when you left I lost a part of

me. It's still so hard to be - lieve. Come back, ba - by, please, 'cause

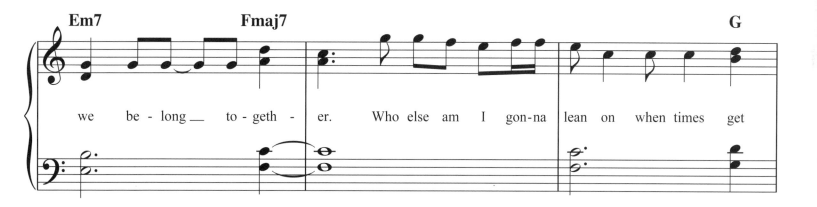

we be - long _____ to - geth - er. Who else am I gon - na lean on when times get

rough? Who's gon - na talk to me on the phone till the sun comes up? Who's _ gon - na take your

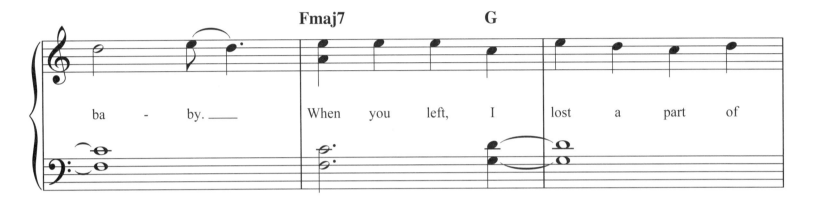

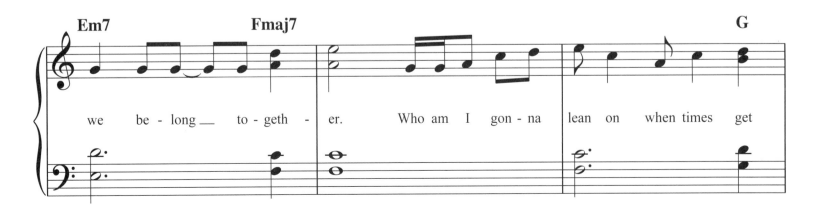

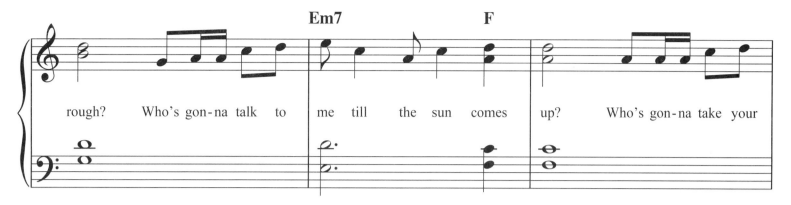

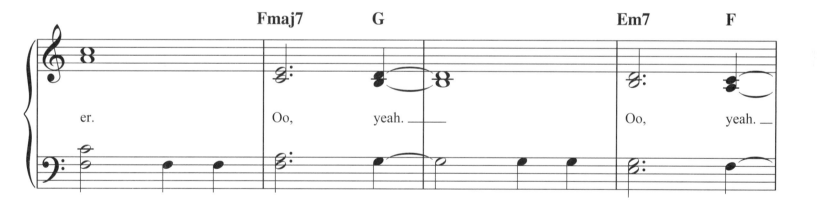

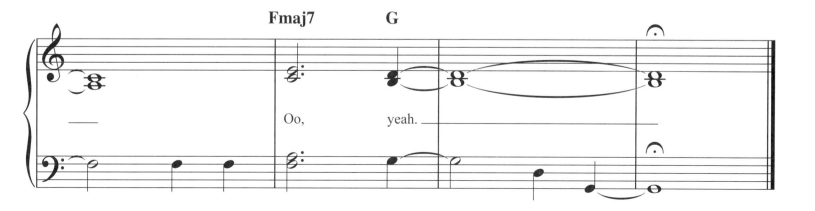

WONDERWALL

Words and Music by
NOEL GALLAGHER

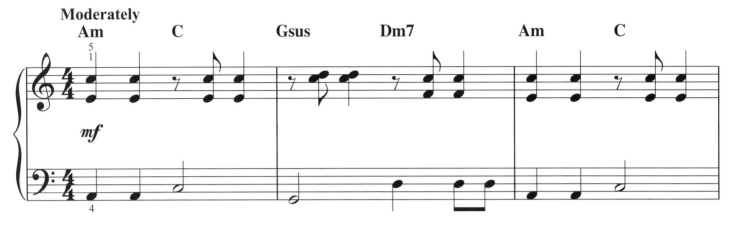

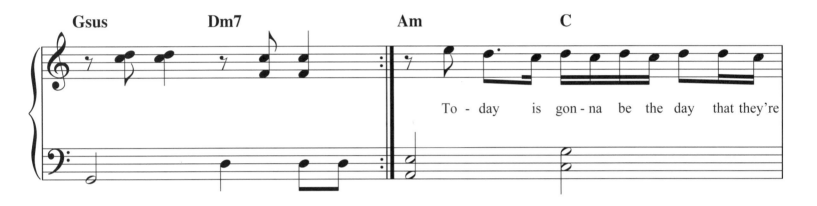

To - day is gon - na be the day that they're

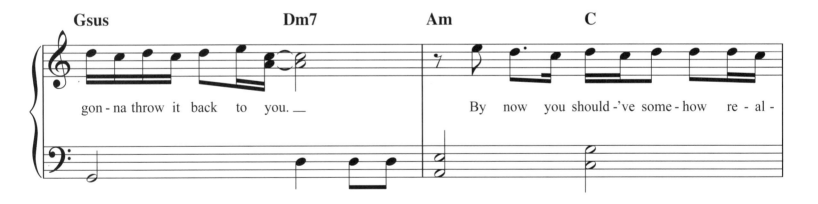

gon - na throw it back to you. ___ By now you should -'ve some - how re - al -

ized what you got - ta do. ___ I don't be - lieve ___ that an - y - bod - y

feels the way I do a-bout you now.

Back - beat the word was on the street that the
To - day was gon-na be the day, but they'll

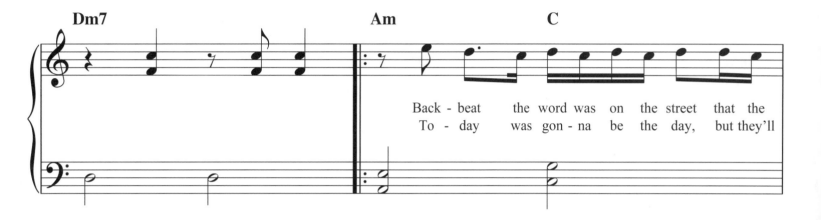

fire __ in your heart is out. __
nev - er throw it back to you. __

I'm sure you've heard it all be-fore, but you
By now you should've some - how re-al-

nev-er real-ly had a doubt. __
ized __ what you're not to do. __

I don't be - lieve __ that an - y-bod - y
I don't be - lieve __ that an - y-bod - y

feels the way I do a - bout you now.
feels the way I do a - bout you now.

And all ___ the roads ___ we have ___ to walk ___ are wind -
And all ___ the roads ___ that lead ___ you there ___ were wind -

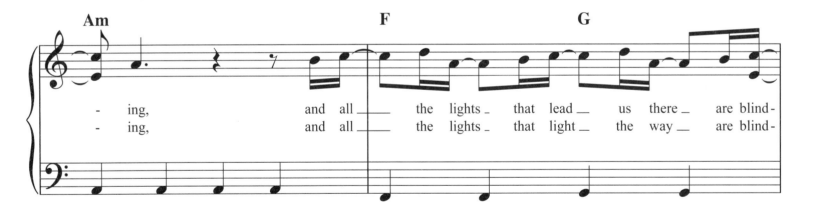

- ing, and all ___ the lights ___ that lead ___ us there ___ are blind -
- ing, and all ___ the lights ___ that light ___ the way ___ are blind -

- ing. There are man - y things ___ that I ___ would
- ing. There are man - y things ___ that I ___ would

like to say to you, __ but I don't know how. _____
like to say to you, __ but I don't know how. _____

Be - cause ⎫
I said ⎭ may - be _____

you're gon - na be the one that saves me, _____

and af - ter all, _____ you're my won - der - wall. _

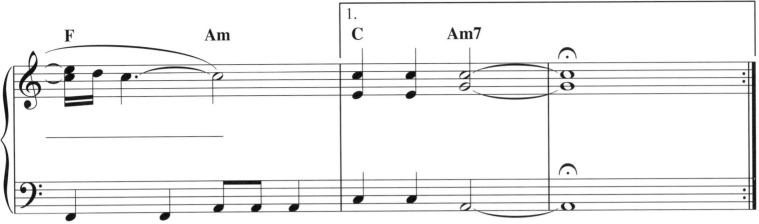

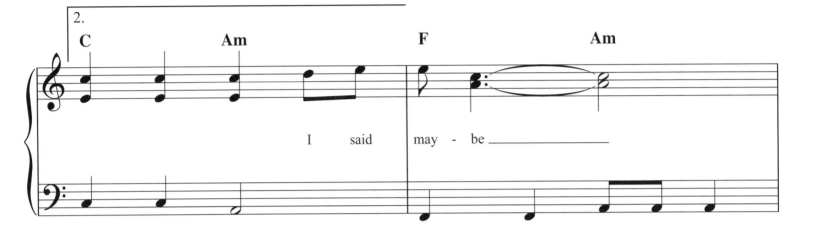

I said may - be

you're gon - na be the one that saves me, ____

and af - ter all, ____ you're my won - der - wall.

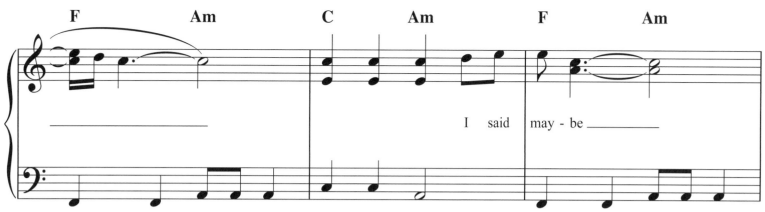

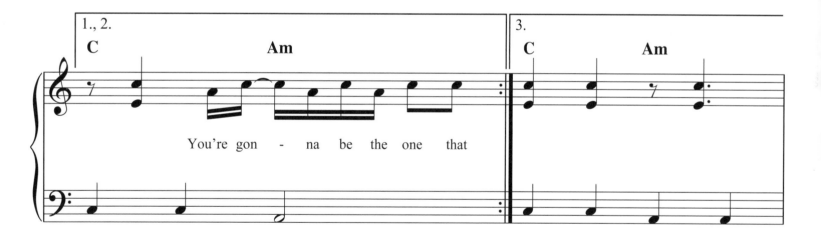

PARTY IN THE U.S.A.

Words and Music by JESSICA CORNISH,
LUKASZ GOTTWALD and CLAUDE KELLY

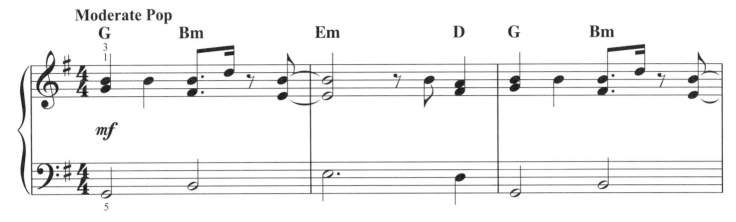

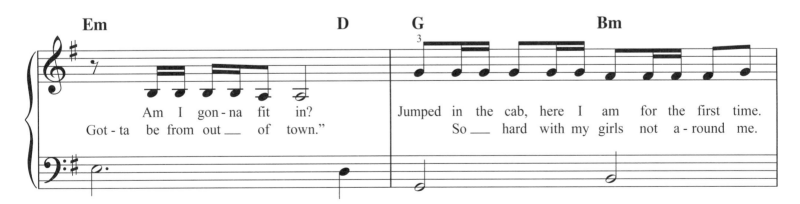

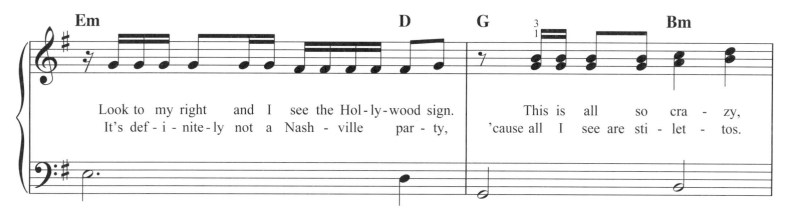

Look to my right   and I   see the Hol-ly-wood sign.   This is all   so   cra-zy,
It's def-i-nite-ly not a Nash-ville   par-ty,   'cause all   I   see are sti-let - tos.

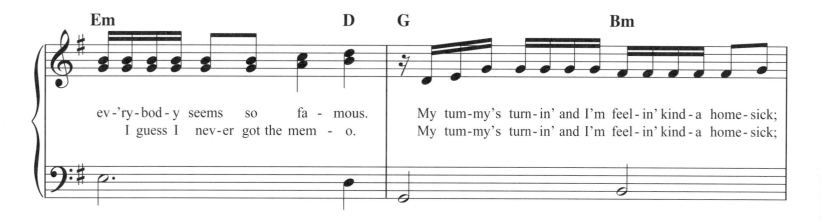

ev-'ry-bod-y seems   so   fa - mous.   My tum-my's turn-in' and I'm feel-in' kind-a home-sick;
I guess I   nev-er got the mem - o.   My tum-my's turn-in' and I'm feel-in' kind-a home-sick;

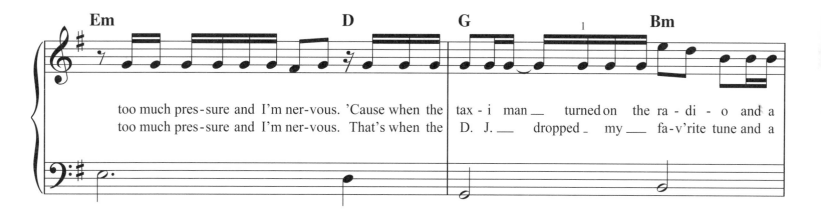

too much pres-sure and I'm ner-vous. 'Cause when the tax-i man __ turned on the ra-di-o and a
too much pres-sure and I'm ner-vous. That's when the D. J. __ dropped __ my __ fa-v'rite tune and a

Jay - Z song was   on.   And the Jay - Z song was   on, _____   and the
Brit - ney song was   on.   And the Brit - ney song was   on, _____   and the

Jay - Z song was on. }
Brit - ney song was on. } So, I put my hands up; they're play-in' my song. The

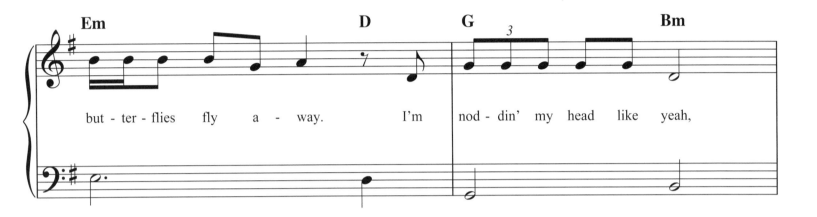

but - ter - flies fly a - way. I'm nod - din' my head like yeah,

mov - in' my hips like yeah. Got my hands up; they're play - in' my song. I know

I'm gon - na be o - kay. Yeah, _____ it's a

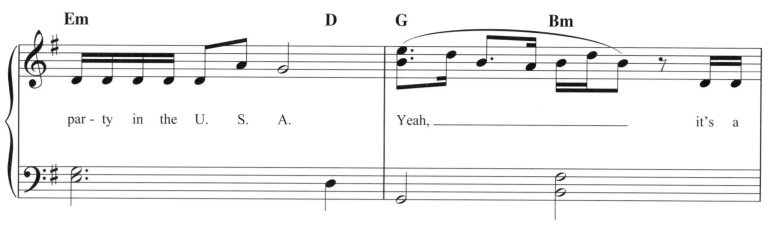

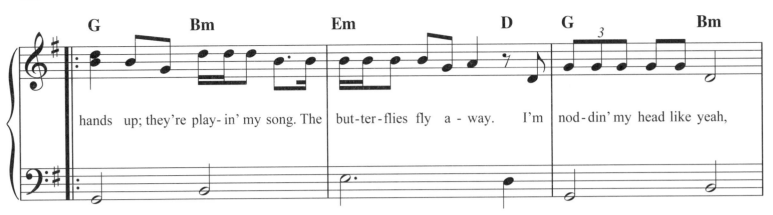

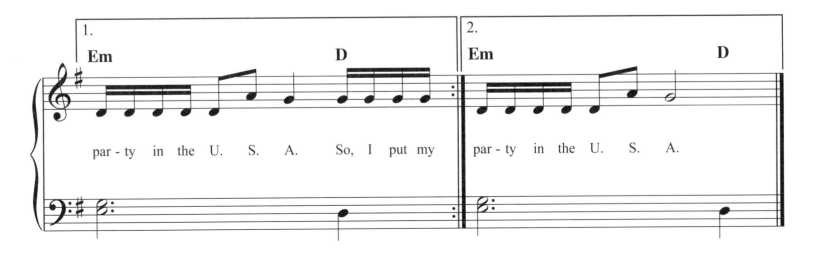